A BRIEF HISTORY OF CENTRAL BANKING

HOW THE QUEST FOR FINANCIAL STABILITY LED TO UNCONVENTIONAL MONETARY PRACTICES

DOMINIC HAYNES

CONTENTS

HOW TO GET A FREE SURPRISE HISTORY EBOOK

Get access to the surprise history ebook below and free and unlimited access to all of my future books by joining my community.

Scan with your camera to join.

INTRODUCTION

While the earliest communities used the barter system of exchanging goods, its loopholes soon showed up when people started traveling in search of new markets and goods to take home. Necessity led to the development of various sizes of coins and metals to provide store value for trade.

With that, banking made its debut when the wealthy realized they needed safe places to store their coins. It helped that ancient empires needed functioning financial systems to make trade possible, collect taxes, and distribute wealth. Since then, banks have been central to a nation's economy. Even so, countries did not always have one authority responsible for all policies affecting their supply of credit and money. Modern central banks developed over time.

Modern central banks have become vital institutions, crucial in shaping and safeguarding the financial landscape. Entrusted with managing a nation's currency and formulating monetary policies, central banks are indispensable to economies worldwide. They play a significant role in promoting stability, fostering economic growth, and safeguarding financial systems. The main objectives of a central bank include:

- Maintaining price stability

One of the primary objectives of central banks is to maintain price stability within an economy. Price stability is about keeping inflation low and stable over an extended period. Central banks achieve this by implementing monetary policies, which include controlling interest rates and managing the money supply. By keeping inflation in check, central banks instill confidence in consumers and businesses, allowing them to make informed financial decisions and plan purchases for the future. Stable prices also provide a predictable environment for long-term planning and investment.

- Implementing monetary policy

Central banks have the authority to formulate and execute monetary policies, making them powerful economic agents. Through monetary policy tools, such as adjusting interest rates, central banks can influence borrowing costs, regulate money supply, and stabilize exchange rates. During economic downturns, central banks can stimulate investment and consumption by lowering interest rates, thus encouraging borrowing and spending. Conversely, during periods of excessive growth, central banks can increase interest rates to cool down the economy and prevent overheating and inflation. The ability to influence economic activity through monetary policy makes central banks critical in promoting stable economic growth.

- Banking and finance supervision

Central banks serve as regulators and supervisors of commercial banks, contributing to the financial system's stability. Central banks ensure that financial institutions operate safely and soundly by setting and enforcing prudential norms and regulations. They conduct regular inspections, stress tests, and risk assessments to identify potential vulnerabilities and prevent systemic risks. In times of financial distress, central banks act as lenders of last resort, providing liquidity to stabilize markets and avoid panic. Their role as the ultimate backstop for the banking system instills confidence among depositors and investors, maintaining the stability of the whole financial system.

- Exchange rate stability

Central banks play a significant role in managing a nation's currency and maintaining exchange rate stability. They hold foreign exchange reserves and intervene in currency markets to influence exchange rates. Stable exchange rates are vital for international trade, reducing uncertainties for exporters and importers. Moreover, a stable currency attracts foreign investments, as it provides confidence in the stability of the investment environment. Central banks' interventions in currency markets help mitigate excessive volatility, ensuring smooth currency flows and bolstering economic growth.

- Promoting financial inclusion

Central banks increasingly recognize the importance of promoting financial inclusion in modern society. Financial inclusion refers to the accessibility and affordability of financial services for all individuals and businesses, including those in underserved communities. Central banks work toward creating an enabling environment that encourages banking penetration, supports digital financial innovation, and extends financial services to marginalized populations. Central banks reduce income inequality by fostering financial inclusion, facilitating economic mobility, and driving sustainable development.

Central banks play a pivotal role in modern society due to their critical functions in maintaining price stability, implementing monetary policies, ensuring financial stability, managing currency, and promoting financial inclusion. Central banks' expertise, independence, and effectiveness have become essential pillars of the global financial system, guiding economies through challenging times and steering them toward prosperity. As guardians of monetary stability and architects of economic growth, central banks are vital institutions that contribute to the overall well-being and stability of nations. This book explores all the forces that shaped the development of modern central banks, following the changes in policies, how we think about money, loaning practices, government, and the influence of these banks on the lives of ordinary citizens.

1

THE ORIGINS OF CENTRAL BANKING:

WHERE IT ALL BEGAN

> *"Let me issue and control a nation's money and I care not who writes the laws."*
>
> — **MAYER AMSCHEL ROTHSCHILD**

You cannot talk about the history of central banking and pay no heed to the development of money and trade. The two are conjoined twins. You will notice the interconnection between them, especially in the cradle days of banking. Some historians claim that the earliest forms of banking as we know it took shape between the 20th and 18th century BC in Mesopotamia and Egypt. Back then, the Assyrian, Babylonian, and Greek merchants needed a way to deposit their gold, take loans, and exchange money. For these traders, the primary need was to keep their gold and money safe. No wonder banking back then happened inside temples considered sacred and safe. This type of lending, more so in Persia and Mesopotamia, would also involve physical goods such as grain, not just gold.

In 1800 BC in Babylon, moneylenders gave loans to farmers and traders. In Rome and Greece, lenders issued loans to people while accepting deposits. Historical records show that they also changed money. The Bible relates a story where Jesus drove money changers and traders out of the temple. There is some argument among historians, with some of them claiming that banking started during the latter part of the 4th millennium BC.

In Asia Minor, for example, the Temple of Artemis has received a lot of notoriety, having been a depository for many historical figures such as Aristotle, Plautus, Caesar, Plutarch, and Xenophon. In the 6th century, the Temple of Apollo served as a gold depository. Other researchers say that the culture of depositing and storing wealth in temples began around 209 BC. Historical evidence shows a temple in Antioch being ransacked for silver and gold. In other parts of the world, like Ancient India, banking traces back to the Vedic period, which started around 1750 BC and expanded during the Maurya dynasty. Lenders used a financial instrument, Adesha, to authorize people to pay certain amounts of money to a third party. In Ancient China, banking arguably developed during the Qin Dynasty.

Across academia, though, historians agree that by 2000 BC, people in different civilizations received loans from lenders who mainly operated from temples and palaces. Records show arguments between borrowers and lenders documented on clay tablets, including the amount of interest expected to be paid. The loans were provided in the form of grains and were scheduled to be repaid after the harvesting season. While historical records may disagree on the timelines, it is almost unanimously agreed that ancient Rome and Greece had the most influence on the development of modern banking.

ANCIENT CIVILIZATIONS AND THEIR BANKING PRACTICES

At its origins, banking is an entrepreneurial activity highly affected by how sophisticated a society is regarding individual ownership and free trade. Most historical records affirm that the foundations for the development of banking in ancient civilizations were provided in ancient Greece. At the time, Greece was allowing private proprietorship separate from state-controlled ownership. The civilization was organized in city-states that encouraged private ownership and citizenship. Financial transactions were undertaken both by public entities and private entrepreneurs.

By 600 BC, Greek lenders had begun creating records of financial transactions. That way, they could facilitate traders and allow them to avoid moving around with large amounts of coins. The idea here was to make transportation and travel more accessible and safer. As a verified trader, you could accept payment in one Greek city, travel, and then receive credit in another city. The Mycenean and Achaean Greeks occupied Asia Minor at the time. It would later be occupied by Ionian Greeks, who all played a significant role in developing banking in its earliest stages. For example, Ephesus, a Greek city-state, housed the Temple of Artemis, Asia's largest depository.

Even though the names changed over time, the Temple of Artemis arguably survived the longest, making it one of the longest-lasting financial institutions. The antiquity lay in modern-day Turkey and stayed between the 7th century BC and AD 400. The enormous building would become one of the Seven Wonders of the Ancient World and an institution honored by people as diverse as Augustus, Alexander, Xerxes, and Croesus. One wonders why it survived that long, and the answers to that question offer wisdom that lends itself to modern banking.

The Temple of Artemis was close to great wealth and existed in a culture that combined trust and fear. It was a holy sanctuary. You messed with the gods at your peril. Ephesus was positioned at the Mediterranean crossroads. As such, the temple enjoyed a wealthy clientele of governors, aristocrats, and kings who valued its security and left their wealth there, where it was out of their enemies' reach. At first, the temple was a place to store wealth under the protection of its deity, the way Xenophon did on his way to join Cyrus the Younger in the 5th century BC. It became more sophisticated as time passed, developing into an international and regional financial institution, operating as a depository and reserve bank, and running a mortgage and fiduciary business.

The Temple of Artemis became so affluent, accumulating so many reserves and earnings, that it was dubbed the Bank of Asia. Religious historians have claimed that one of the significant reasons for its longevity was the fact that it had a higher purpose. It did not just carry out sophisticated banking functions. It was a place where people offered sacred service to a goddess who valued a robust ethical code. It has been argued that banks today also need a guiding purpose and a robust code of ethics to maintain high standards and be sustainable in the future.

Leadership was critical in the early days of banking in Greece. In the Temple of Artemis, governance was characterized by 'godly' levels of collective and personal accountability. The people valued connection and trust. Overall, the temple's leadership passed from the joint supervision of the high priestess and the high priest to the sole charge of a high priest during the Roman empire—an experiment that did not endure but is worth discussing. It is worth noting that Greek lenders clearly understood the risks involved in their business. History suggests that the banks deployed their capital and depository funds with yearly mortgage interest. The money the goddess protected had to stay inviolable, so the bank only gave out 'prime' mortgages and took first-class risks.

Today, transparency and clarity are fundamentals for the public to have confidence in our financial system. These values trace back to the Greeks and were partly responsible for the long-term stability of the Temple of Artemis, even though they did not keep it forever. The temple was plundered and ransacked by the Goths in AD 263, and it finally gave in to the proscription of pagan worship. At this point, the region was now mostly Roman Christian. The following centuries saw the Temple of Artemis preserve some of its reputation. In 1870, an English architect rediscovered its remains so that today regulators and bankers can pay homage to an institution that crystalized the foundations of modern banking.

Some archeological evidence suggests that similar forms of lending were happening in Ancient China and India simultaneously. In India, for example, there is literature from the Vedic times and from the Jatakas that supplies evidence of the existence of bankers or Srethis. From the laws of Manu, it appears moneylending and the associated problems were significant in ancient India. There is one record of people debating interest rates and their role in banking as a business.

Back then, interest rates were prescribed by Hindu lawgivers Vasistha, Gautama, Kautilya, and Yajnavalkya, among others. There was a standard base number of 15% per year. Incidentally, this rate exceeds many banks' current Prime Lending Rate (PLR). It was not as if anyone could get the loans, though. Like in Greece, the loans were only given to prime borrowers, and the basis was different. Vasistha and Manu, two prominent Hindu lawgivers, stipulated that the rates should not vary based on the risk involved or the purpose of borrowing. However, they could be varied based on the caste of the borrowers. The Brahmin were to pay 2%, Vaishya 4%, Kshatriya 3%, and so forth per month.

By the same logic, Chanakya's interest rate structure would be weighed against the risk involved in the borrower's business as long as it worked out to 15% per year for general advances. Traders received the highest rates of 60% per year. In cases where merchandise had to go through forests, traders were forced to pay as much as 120% per year, while the people who moved their goods through the sea had to pay 240% per year. In the same vein, not everyone could be involved in banking. It was reserved only for men within the Vaishya caste.

Regarding debt recovery and disputes, how they were handled was governed by Hindu law. There were specified punishments by caste in disputes arising from loan repayments. The law specified up to 18 types of disputes. For example, whenever a creditor sued a debtor for not paying back, it was the king's duty to ensure the money was repaid. The king was allowed to use all possible means, whether fair or not, to recover the dues. Some records show instances where debtors were tortured or had their wives, cattle, and children killed. The view held was that the defaulter could never absolve himself of debt, even by death. In some places, sons had to pay interest to service the debt left by their fathers. Wives, however, were exempt from the debt incurred by their husbands if they had not consented to his borrowings. However, husbands were liable to repay their wife's debts in all circumstances.

The records of banking in ancient India and China are limited and far apart, which is why the generally accepted timeline is that banking originated in the final decades of the 18th century. The oldest bank in India, for example, was begun in 1806. These facts led historians to concentrate mainly on banking in ancient Greece and the Roman Empire because they were the major shaping forces. During the period of the Roman Empire, there was a significant adoption of Greek banking practices and systematization of banking at a regulatory and administrative level. By the 2nd century AD, bank transactions that involved the payment of debts were notarized so that they could be considered legitimate transactions.

The Romans were expert administrators and builders, and as such, they extricated banking from the temples, making it into a formalized institution with its own distinct buildings. At the time, moneylenders were still profiting like loan sharks do today, but most banking for legitimate businesses and nearly all government spending were done via an institutional bank. Some historical records show that it was Julius Caesar who began the practice of allowing bankers to take over someone's land instead of loan payments. This practice was a significant power shift in the relationship between a debtor and a creditor. Before this, landed noblemen had been untouchable, passing on their debts to their descendants until their lineage or that of the creditor died out.

Historical records support that while banking was transitioning from temples into formalized institutions, bankers would still loan out money to people in addition to keeping it safe. Since coins are smaller than other mediums of trade, they could be exchanged and hoarded more quickly than, say, 300-pound pigs. It made sense that soon enough, the wealthy class of merchants also took up lending coins to people who needed them. With that, temples started handling only large loans, including those given to different sovereigns. Since devout priests and workers always occupied temples and were regularly patrolled by soldiers, it took a while for society to accept formalized banking institutions as being equally safe or safer than temples. There was a period when both temples and formal banks fought for the business of the people.

It didn't help that temples did not pay interest on deposits but charged their borrowers interest on loans. They were also involved in currency validation and exchange. There were thousands of them scattered throughout Roman territories, so phasing them out in favor of private repositories was not easy. Some temples, like the Temple of Saturn, were so prestigious that they housed the empire's public treasuries. Others, like the Temple of Juno Moneta, were mints.

By the 3rd century BC, commerce had developed a great deal throughout the Mediterranean, and trade was expanding to new foreign markets—factors that helped banking to continue growing in the Roman world. Besides temples, another group of people also dabbled in providing banking services to people. These money changers would set up their bases in stalls and shops in the forum to serve the average earners. Because of their target clientele, money changers saw their role gain greater importance even as commerce developed toward the mid-century. As mentioned earlier, Greek banking practices greatly influenced how banking developed in the Roman world, and the money changers were another example of this. They shaped their services around the methods of the trapezius (from the Greek word *trapeze,* which means counter), who provided banking services in counting houses around the forum. The term trapezius would later be replaced by the Latin terms *mensarii* and *argentarii* (drawing from the Latin word for the 'bank').

In general, there were three types of people in Rome who conducted banking activities—the *argentarii,* the *nummular,* and the *mensarii.* The *argentarii* were private persons or free citizens who did not have state oversight in their service provisions. They were part of a guild that accepted only a select number of new members every year. Their primary function was exchanging currency from foreign currencies into the Roman currency (*permutatio*). They had established stalls and shops around the forum, rented from the state. With time, their role expanded, adding money transactions like lending money, holding money, taking part in auctions, and determining the value of coins. Some *argentarii* also dabbled in detecting forged coins and circulating newly minted money. Their job greatly resembled that of the modern-day bank.

Unexpectedly, given their target clientele and their diversity, the *argentarii* grew to be very respected. It is argued that the exclusivity with which the members of the parent guild were chosen helped. Some members of the *argentarii* were from the upper class, usually the group of people doing large-scale business for the very wealthy. A few were looked down upon because of their high rates and the fact that they did business on a small scale, but generally speaking, the reputation of the few did not cloud the whole *argentarii*.

The Roman currency, permutation, was done for a small fee. The *argentarii* would dabble with this and later become involved in bills of exchange. In those cases, they received a sum of money, for instance, to be paid in Athens, then they drew a bill that would be payable there by another banker. Much like today, they needed to be aware of the exact value of a foreign coin in different places and at different times. Their job also involved keeping money deposited by other people and making payments on their behalf, the same way modern banks do. These payments were made on the owner's word. The owner had to use a prescription or check to make the payment, and whenever two people were involved in a transaction using the same *argentarii*, the *argentarii* would record it in books called codices. The codices accurately recorded every transaction, date, and the involved parties. The records were considered documents of very high authority, so much so that they would be used in the justice courts as evidence beyond question.

If you only made a deposit into the bank, the *argentarius* did not pay interest. The only time they paid interest was on the money you deposited and allowed them to use in other lucrative transactions, like loaning people money. You would often see *argentarii* in public auctions or spot them participating in commercial transactions. They were nearly always present in those auctions on behalf of other people's interests, receiving payments and recording the people involved in different transactions, items sold, and how much they were sold for. In commercial transactions, the *argentarii* came in as agents for any of the involved parties. Sometimes they represented the seller, and other times the purchaser. They were so influential that they could be involved in selling a person's entire estate. In cases involving large payments, people depended on the *argentarii* to make the transactions legit.

Another group of bankers in the Roman world was the *mensarii*. *Mensarii* were the public bankers of the time. The state often appointed them and would take authority in exceptional circumstances, like during periods of war or when there was general poverty. Their job was to help the plebeians or commoners deal with economic difficulties and ease social unrest. It should be noted that in ancient Rome, if plebeians were in debt and could not fulfill that debt, they could be punished by slavery. The first record of the *mensarii* puts them around 352 BCE. There was a commission of *mensarii,* made up of five men appointed by the public bank and given the job of addressing the debt of citizens. This commission covered the citizens who could provide security for their debt from public resources. Those who could not had to give their property to creditors after public officials did a reliable valuation of the property.

Later on, around 216 BCE, a law governing the operation of the *mensarii* was passed. By law, the commission of *mensarii* could have three people. They would do the same job as the five-person commission. According to some historical records, some of the roles of the *mensarii* resembled those of the *argentarii*. During economic distress, it is said that it was difficult to tell the two apart. For example, the *mensarii* had a job of holding deposits, such as the payments made to soldiers, valuing coins, and determining their authenticity. Generally speaking, though, their role was considered to be positive because they were able to deal with the issues of excess debt within the Roman economy. Some notable *mensarii* of the time whose names still echo the halls of banking and history today include Quintus Publius and Titus Emilius.

The final group of bankers in ancient Rome was the *nummularii*. These were officers of the mint, with their primary function revolving around testing the quality of new coins. They controlled a bank whose job was to introduce new coins into the market and take old or foreign coins to exchange them for new ones. Like the *mensarii* and the *argentarii*, they also tested coins to determine their authenticity, especially when participating in large transactions. They had a job description similar to that of the *argentarii*—they changed money, lent it out, held deposits, executed sales, and made payments on behalf of clients. They also carried out property auctions according to different wills, made payments to foreign places through local banks, and maintained a codex that could be used in the courts.

Banking became more sophisticated in the Roman world as trade expanded, economies grew, and the empire's influence expanded. Eventually, temples were phased out as repositories for money, and public institutions took over. The *argentarii* grew in their influence, participating in more banking activities as trade in the Roman world expanded. In the modern world, the *argentarii* would be bankers. The *mensarii* helped to deal with the indebtedness of the commoners. In today's world, they could be likened to 'bad banks' that are set up to deal with nonperforming loans. The *nummularii* were officers of the mint whose job centered around circulating new coins, something also done by modern-day banks. It is remarkable how widespread the use of loans was and how complex and developed banking activities were in the Roman world. Banking contributed significantly to the growth of trade and commerce and the creation of ancient Rome's wealth.

Eventually, the Roman Empire crumbled and took some of its banking practices with it. Some banking institutions lived on in the Middle Ages through the services of the Knights Templar and the papal bankers. There were also small-time moneylenders who competed with the church. The adoption of banking in the post-Roman world was delayed by different restrictions on interest prescribed by different religions. For instance, the Hebrew Bible's Torah was against earning any interest from deposits, which was a common practice of lenders. The Jews were not allowed to charge any interest on loans they gave to other Jews. However, they were under obligation to charge interest on loans provided to non-Jews.

In the same way, the Israelites were not permitted to charge interest on loans given to fellow Israelites. In the early days, Christianity and other prominent religions banned usury, a factor that delayed the adoption of banking. In the 16th century, Protestantism was on the rise, which weakened religious restrictions on interest and freed up the development of banking.

After the fall of the Roman Empire, there was a significant decrease in banking activities as Christianity rose and curtailed some banking practices, citing them as immoral. The banking profession was facing restrictions. Banks temporarily disappeared after the collapse of the Roman Empire, but the idea of banking came up again in the 12th and 13th centuries in Italy, mainly in Genoa and Florence.

THE RISE OF MODERN CENTRAL BANKING IN EUROPE

During the Middle Ages, merchants in Genoa, Florence, and to some extent, Venice helped create new techniques for trade. In turn, these techniques shaped modern banking. At the time, the church had sanctioned military campaigns—the Crusades—meant to conquer the Middle East. These Crusades required a lot of financial backing. Because of that, rulers like Henry II of England started taxing people to fund the cause. It is also said that Henry used knightly crusading orders such as the Templars and Hospitallers as his bankers in the Middle East, then called the Holy Land. Essential merchant cities like Venice and Genoa sometimes took part in the Crusades directly by offering workforce or using their fleets. Between 1095 and 1099 AD, for example, the Genoese merchants were involved in the Crusade, as were the Venetians in the Fourth Crusade in 1204 AD.

The Italian merchants from Genoa and Venice used maritime and land trade routes to operate in the Middle East, North Africa, Asia, and Europe. However, they were prominent in their industry because of their dominant positions in the Mediterranean, Black Seas, and Adriatic Seas. Their ambitious leadership had seen to it that their merchant fleets were well established. First, the merchants would partner with local people to raise capital. These partnerships allowed them to pay for everything they needed, including ships, wages for the crew, the goods they needed to trade, and supplies for their journey. Since these merchants dealt with vast sums of money, they started finding people they trusted to leave some of it with.

Other than partnerships, the merchants also relied on the use of credit. It helped that the amount of cash circulating at the time was insufficient to develop trade, so it became safer to use promissory notes or bills of exchange. These notes helped to hide the interest that was charged on loans. It could be hidden by misrepresenting it as a foreign currency transaction. This was done to escape 'punishment' from the church. Finally, merchants sought insurance for their trips to protect themselves from pirates or poor weather. Since their journeys often faced many forms of danger, they had to deal with very high insurance costs.

The fourth significant way that the Genoese and Florentine merchants helped develop banking in Europe was through the development of accounting. At the time, they relied on double-entry bookkeeping to track their profits and losses. This type of accounting helps track debts or money spent and credits or money earned as well as assets and liabilities. These practices, from using deposits and charging interest to lending money on credit, led to the development of the banking we know today. Some historians argue that, beyond the evolution of banking, the Italians were responsible for the first-ever books to include vocabulary that was trade-related to different languages. Their books had information about other commercial practices and trade routes. It helped that Italian city-states like Florence and Genoa were also prominent in education in advanced mathematics.

During the Renaissance, banking in Europe continued to grow. Major European centers in places like Florence were becoming more influential alongside banking families like the Medici. The Medici family, also referred to as the House of Medici, shaped banking in the European Renaissance. The wealthy banking family also enjoyed a lot of political power between the 14th and 16th centuries. For example, they produced four popes, including Pope Pius IV and many political leaders in Florence. They also contributed French queens, including Marie de Medici and Catherine de Medici.

As is often the case with influential people in history, the Medici family rose to fill the vacuum when another wealthy Italian banking family, the Bonsignoris, declared bankruptcy. At the time, the most significant banking center across Europe was Siena. Because of the bankruptcy of the Bonsignoris family, Florence became Italy's leading financial center. The Medici family lived in Florence—and banking played a significant role in their rise to power. Between 1397 and 1494, they established one of Europe's most significant and famous banks, the Medici Bank. Like Italian merchants, the bank utilized the newest developments of its time, such as double-entry bookkeeping. Other banks that appeared in Europe around the same time include the Taula de Canvi, Barcelona, the Banco di Napoli, Naples, the Bank of Saint George in Genoa, and the Fugger Bank in Augsburg.

It is argued that modern banking truly emerged at the end of the 16th century. The culture of taking deposits, transferring funds, changing money, and lending it started to disappear. These financial practices often involved issuing bank debt rather than silver and gold coins. New banking practices enhanced industrial and commercial growth by offering a safe, convenient, and fast means of payment. Toward the end of the 17th century, banks started participating in funding European wars. The trend meant that the government got more involved in banking and started imposing regulations. Soon enough, central banks began to appear, and the success of the new banking system in

London and Amsterdam started spreading to other European states.

Banking practices further developed in England during the 17th century. Wealthy merchants started depositing their gold with the London goldsmiths and received a receipt indicating the purity and quantity of their gold. They could use these receipts to get their gold, but they had to do so in person. They could not send someone to collect on their behalf. At the time, goldsmiths owned private vaults that they used for storage. They charged a small storage fee to the merchants. As this system expanded, people started to trade using notes rather than coins as they found the notes to be safer.

During the 18th century, banks expanded their service offerings to include checks, protection from overdrafting, clearing facilities, and security investments. Checks were first used in the 1600s, and by the 1800s, they had become an internationally accepted payment mode. The industrial revolution contributed a lot to the development of banking because industries necessitated the expansion of the financial system. Before the industrial revolution started, silver and gold were the preferred modes of trade for businesses. During that period, you could find three tiers of banks in England—the Bank of England, county banks, and private banks. The Bank of England was founded in 1694 by William of Orange and would later become the storage for the country's gold.

Private banks were used to offer financial services to industrialists and merchants, while county banks, which were only available in local areas, served everyone else. This was happening at a time when entrepreneurship was proliferating. Capitalists, financiers, merchants, and sales clerks embraced entrepreneurship and changed how companies were owned and run. Joint-stock companies and shareholders in companies became a thing, which increased the demand for capital. Similarly, there was a high demand for infrastructure, and companies needed money to fund their daily operations. Rapid business growth created a need for a money repository and a source of development loans. As a result, particular banks appeared to service the market while profiting from the difference between interest earned on loans and interest paid on deposits.

Around the same period, the Swedish Riksbank was established. The bank was founded in 1668 as a joint-stock bank with twofold functions. First, the bank would be able to lend to the government. Secondly, it worked as a trade clearinghouse. After the success of the Bank of England and the Riksbank, many other central banks were set up in different parts of Europe. For example, in 1800, Napoleon set up the Banque de France, whose job was to give money to the government and stabilize the currency. Early central banks used notes as their primary currency. They also functioned as banks for bankers because they could facilitate transfers between different banks. In the early 20th century, the Federal Reserve, for example, was established in the US to offer financial stability and consolidate various forms of currency used in commerce.

Scattered throughout the development of central banks was another influential family, the Rothschild family. Historically, this family was seen as a major source of loans to the Bank of England. In 1804, the family bank started trading on the London Stock Exchange and, five years later, got into the gold business. The family immensely helped the development of significant world railway systems and provided financing to governments for different projects, including the construction of the Suez Canal. During the Russo-Japanese War, the family funded Japan and, later on, the French Empire.

During the founding periods of modern banking, promissory notes were used as the primary mode of financial transactions. The London goldsmiths had popularized them. As mentioned earlier, goldsmiths gave people receipts after making a deposit. The receipt included details like the quality and quantity of gold deposited. Later, they morphed into promissory notes, used by merchants in business transactions as money. Credit cards were introduced soon after to deal with the issue of mistaken identity and fraud. In 1928, the charge plate was created, having information such as the owner's name, city, and state of the customer. Only large merchants could get access to credit cards. Each one had a small paper card at the back where the merchants could record their transactions.

It was not until 1950 that the founders of Diners Club expanded the concept of using credit cards in business transactions. These two men, Ralph Schneider and Frank McNamara, developed the first charge card. Eight years later, the American Express card was introduced by Carte Blanche, leading to the creation of a worldwide credit card network.

The history of central banking in Europe has roots in ancient Greece and Rome. Prominent families, including the Medici and Rothschild families, played defining roles in the growth of banking. In the ancient world, merchants and farmers got loans from lenders based in temples. They changed their money there and made deposits. Things changed during the Renaissance in Italy when the Peruzzi and Medici families created banks that issued loans and took deposits, fashioned after the Roman public banking depositories. These families were responsible for the spread of banking and the rise of central banking in Europe and other parts of the world. The Industrial Revolution helped speed things up because entrepreneurs needed large amounts of capital for their operations. Central banks helped to regulate banks and fund government projects.

HOW CENTRAL BANKS BECAME THE GUARDIANS OF FINANCIAL STABILITY

Many forces were behind the development of banking and modern central banks. A central bank is an authority responsible for the policies affecting a country's supply and cost of credit and money. A central bank uses its monetary policy tools—discount window lending, open market operations, and so forth—to affect the interest rates in the short term and the monetary base to achieve important policy goals. Today, modern monetary policy has three goals. First, it is concerned about price stability or stabilizing the value of money. This means maintaining a consistent inflation rate. Secondly, it deals with stabilizing an economy, often seen as low unemployment and sustainable growth rates. You can also interpret this as creating a policy to smooth the business cycle and dampen economic shocks. Finally, monetary policy is about financial stability, which encompasses well-running payment systems and the prevention of financial crises.

One might think central banks have always existed to perform this job, but that is far from the truth. In the 17th century, when the Swedish Riksbank was established, things were slightly different. Later on, when the bank was chartered, the goal was to be able to lend money to the government and to be a clearinghouse for commerce. Decades later, when the Bank of England was set up, the goal was to buy government debt. Other central banks that came up around that time served the same purpose. A few, like Napoleon's Banque de France, were established to solve monetary disarray. These early central banks had a monopoly over private note issues, but even though they helped governments, they were also private entities that participated in other banking activities. Since they kept deposits for other banks and facilitated bank-to-bank transactions, they seemed to have a natural authority. They became a repository for most banks, which allowed them to become a lender of last resort in the face of a financial crisis. In other words, central banks could offer emergency cash to their correspondents during economic distress.

As mentioned earlier, some central banks were established to serve as clearinghouses. In any decent-sized city, many banks would come together to economize the costs of giving checks to each other. Rather than having each bank send a clerk directly to other banks, they would send a pair of clerks to a central location. This central location was a clearinghouse. One clerk from each bank would move around desks, presenting many checks in succession to clerks from other banks. The sitting clerk would tally the checks presented, and after that was complete, they would collate and reconcile all the tally sheets. After the process, every bank would either have an amount they owed the clearinghouse, which would go to other banks, or they would have an amount due from the clearinghouse. The settlements would be done that day, or the balance would be carried over to the next day.

Clearinghouses were a significant feature even before the Federal Reserve System. As you will find out later on, many Fed banks were modeled after these clearinghouses. What's important to note is that banks that were members of a clearinghouse were often owed funds by the clearinghouse. As a result, member banks were very interested in the financial health of other member banks. Clearinghouses were responsible for setting membership standards, and required financial statements and regular member bank audits. In other words, they worked like regulation and supervision agencies, the same way federal agencies do today.

It is worth noting that member banks owned the clearinghouses. Each of those banks would provide one member of the board of directors, and this team would set rules and policies to oversee the clearinghouse operations. Clearinghouses worked well in cities where sending couriers daily to a central location was convenient. However, outside cities, in remotely located banks, there was a different institutional mechanism for clearing checks known as correspondent banking. In this system, these banks had relationships with other banks—correspondents. If such a bank received a check from a distant bank, it would send a correspondent to pick up the money for them. In the same way, if a city correspondent got a check from a remote bank, they would send someone to collect payment.

While the Federal Reserve System belongs to a wave of central banks that emerged in the 20th century, its job was to consolidate different instruments that people were using for currency and to offer financial stability. By this stage, most countries had adopted the gold standard. As you will see in Chapter III, the gold standard prevailed until 1914 and had each country define its currency based on a fixed weight of gold. Central banks had large reserves of gold that helped ensure that their notes could be turned into gold as required. When their reserves failed to balance because of payment deficits or other domestic circumstances, they would increase their discount rates to other banks. This would raise interest rates and, in turn, attract foreign investment, bringing more gold into the country.

Central banks kept to the gold standard rule above all other considerations. The ability to convert notes into gold was the economy's nominal anchor. That is to say that the amounts that banks could supply were constrained by the value of gold in the reserve, which also determined the price level. Since the price level was connected to known commodities, whose value was shaped by market forces, the expectation of the future price level was also connected. In this sense, too, central banks were firmly committed to price stability. They were not so worried about the stability of the real economy because they were constrained to operate under the gold standard.

In this period, the banks started serving as lenders of last resort during periods of financial stress—when events like bad harvests, wars, or defaults by railroad companies created a scramble for liquidity. This started in the 19th century as a consequence of the response of the Bank of England to such panics. At the time, together with other banks, the Bank of England would protect its reserves first, meaning it didn't help correspondents in need. Of course, this created major panics in 1825, 1837, 1847, and so on, leading to much criticism for the bank. In response to the criticism, the bank created a responsibility doctrine that required it to hold its private interests in service of the public interests of the system as a whole. This new rule allowed the bank to lend freely as long as there was given sound collateral and a penalty rate above the market rates to prevent a moral hazard.

Modern central banks did not care much about domestic economic stability at their inception, but the First World War changed things. The shift reflected a change in the economies of many countries—labor movements were increasing, for example, and there were restrictions on migrations. A few years later, central banks started paying attention to external (gold prices and reserves) and internal (employment, prices, and output) stability. The new responsibility doctrine fully ushered central banks into their role as the guardians of financial stability.

2

THE GREAT DEPRESSION:

HOW CENTRAL BANKS SAVED THE WORLD

> *"The only thing we have to fear is fear itself."*
>
> — **FRANKLIN D. ROOSEVELT**

If you have a family member or know someone who lived through the Great Depression, you have likely heard stories about it at the dinner table. It was a period of hunger marches and protests. Unionism spread like wildfire. People suffered, some quietly, feeling the deep shame of their poverty. Regardless of their situation, the Great Depression changed everyone who survived it. During those years, some places were hit harder than others. Unemployment was high. Cities were segregated. The trouble was immense.

According to history books and economists, the Great Depression describes a period of worldwide economic downturn that started in 1929 and lasted for ten years to 1939, making it the most prolonged and most severe depression ever to be experienced in the Western world. It sparked significant changes in economic institutions, shaping economic theory and forging microeconomic policy. Even though it started in the United States, it caused substantial declines in output, acute deflation, and severe unemployment in nearly every country in the world. Its cultural and social effects were just as staggering, especially in the US, where its effect came second only to the impact of the Civil War.

As you look through the history books of different countries, you will notice a discrepancy between when the Great Depression started, but that is because it varied substantially across countries. It was exceptionally long and more severe in Europe and the US. It was experienced a bit less in Latin America and Japan. Perhaps, unsurprisingly, the depression stemmed from many different causes, including things like financial panics, declines in consumer demand, and misguided government policies. The gold standard, which linked almost all the countries in the world in a network of fixed currency exchange rates, contributed to the transmission of the depression from America to other countries of the world.

It makes sense, therefore, that the recovery from the depression would be tied to the abandonment of the gold standard, which will be touched on in this chapter, but primarily discussed in Chapter III. Recovery was also connected to the subsequent monetary expansion. Still, the economic impacts of the Great Depression were extreme, including profound changes in economic policy and a lot of human suffering. Between March and May of 1929, the United States was experiencing what was seen as an ordinary recession. Later on, the recession became markedly worse and continued until 1933. During that period, prices and output fell precipitously. At the peak of the downturn, in the US, industrial production had reduced by 47% while the country's GDP had decreased by 30%. The wholesale price index went down 33% —deflation.

There is some debate among economists and historians about the reliability of the statistics obtained during the Great Depression. Still, it is widely agreed that all over the world, unemployment rates were the highest they have ever been. If you compare the statistics for the Great Depression in the US with those of the Financial Crisis of 2007 to 2009, the Great Depression takes the day by a whopping 208% increase in unemployment rates.

Practically, every country in the world was affected. Great Britain struggled with a recession and low growth during the majority of the second half of the 1920s. It may not have slipped into a severe depression until the early 1930s, when it saw a peak reduction in industrial production. For France, the economic downturn was also relatively short in the early 1930s. The country saw a short-lived recovery in the two years that followed, but its industrial production and prices reduced substantially between 1933 and 1936. In Germany, the economy entered a downturn at the beginning of 1928 and then became stable for a few months before falling again toward the end of 1929. Germany saw a decrease in industrial production nearly equal to what the US experienced.

In Latin America, a few countries also fell into depression in late 1928 and 1929, just before the US's output declined. Some less developed countries like Brazil and Argentina experienced mild downturns. Essentially, the general deflation in price that was being felt in the US was also present in other countries. Practically, every industrialized state had to deal with declines in wholesale prices in the years following 1929. Japan had a flexible price structure then, meaning deflation was unusually rapid up to 1931. This rapid deflation may have helped to temper the decline in production in the country. The prices dropped dismally for primary commodities that were traded in world markets. For example, the prices of silk, cotton, rubber, and coffee were lowered by more than $50 between 1929 and 1930. As a result, the terms of trade also declined, affecting the producers of these commodities.

In the US, recovery from the Great Depression started in 1933. By the mid-1930s, outputs proliferated, and real GDP started increasing at an average rate of 9% annually. Output had declined precipitously in the early 1930s, and even such momentous increases meant it remained well below the long-run trend path. The country would suffer another downturn between 1937 and 1938. It was not until 1942 that the country's output returned to its long-run trend path.

For the rest of the world, recovery varied the same way the start of the economic downturn did. The British economy stopped declining when Great Britain abandoned the gold standard in 1931, for example, but its genuine recovery started a year later. For several Latin American countries, recovery began in the early months of 1932. Both Japan and Germany started recovering in the fall of 1932. Canada and other smaller European countries began reviving their economies in 1933, while France, which experienced the depression later than most countries, started recovering in 1938.

THE STOCK MARKET CRASH

Fundamentally, the Great Depression in the US was caused by a reduction in spending, often called aggregate demand, which caused a decline in production as merchandisers and manufacturers noticed unintended increases in their inventories. Of course, the reasons people spent less during the depression varied over time. As mentioned earlier, this decline was passed on to the rest of the world through the gold standard. However, there were other factors influencing the downturn in different countries. In the US, for example, the story would be incomplete if it did not touch on the stock market crash of 1929. This crash is said to have started from a tight monetary policy that was meant to limit stock market speculation.

To understand this, we have to step back a few years. The 1920s were generally a prosperous decade, even though the boom was not exceptional. Prices stayed constant for a large proportion of the decade. There had been mild recessions in 1924 and 1927, but their influence was insignificant. In 1921, the stock prices registered a record low before rising fourfold to peak in 1929. Between 1928 and 1929, the Federal Reserve raised interest rates, hoping to slow the stock price increases. The higher interest rates made life difficult for interest-sensitive spenders in industries like automobile and construction. In turn, that reduced production. Some scholars believe that the housing construction boom of the 1920s created an excess supply of housing and a significant drop in construction between 1928 and 1929.

By 1929, stock prices in the US had gotten to levels that could not be justified by any reasonable anticipations of earnings in the future. Consequently, when some minor events led to price declines toward the end of 1929, investors lost confidence in the stock market, and the bubble burst. On a day that has come to be called Black Thursday, the 24th of October 1929, panic selling started. Many stocks were bought on margin—that is, they were purchased using loans obtained by a small percentage of the value of the stock. Because of this, the price reductions forced some investors to make their holdings liquid, creating another price drop. According to the Cowles Index, between their peak in September and their lowest in November, stock prices had reduced by 33%. This decline was so dramatic and unheard of that it is often called the Great Crash of 1929.

The stock market crash also substantially contributed to reduced aggregate demand in the US. People stopped buying durable goods and investing in businesses. A possible explanation is that the crisis made people uncertain about their future income. In turn, that caused firms and consumers to postpone their purchases of durable goods. Even though the loss of wealth triggered by the reduction in stock prices was low, the crash may also have reduced spending by causing people to feel poorer. Because of the reduced business and consumer spending, actual output in the US, which had been reducing up to this point, fell rapidly throughout 1930. Thus, even though the Great Depression and the great stock market crash are separate events, the latter was a contributing factor to the declines in unemployment and panic in the US.

BANKING PANICS

Another blow to aggregate demand in the US was the banking panics that started in the fall of 1930. It is important to note that these panics were happening in banks all over the world as well. A banking panic starts when many people who had previously deposited their money lose confidence in their banks' solvency and demand that their bank pays returns their cash. Typically, banks only hold a fraction of their deposits as cash reserves. In a panic, they are forced to liquidate their loans so that they raise the required cash. That fast liquidation process can cause a previously solvent bank to fail. The US experienced many of these banking panics from 1930 through to 1932. The final wave of panics endured until 1933 and culminated with the president declaring a national 'bank holiday.' During the bank holiday, all banks were closed, and they could resume work only after government inspectors deemed them solvent.

Banking panics took a severe toll on global banking systems. Over 20% of banks in the United States failed within a year. Banking panics tend to be primarily irrational and inexplicable, but some factors contribute to the problem, which can be explained. According to economic historians, the 1920s saw a noteworthy increase in farm debt which worked alongside the US policies of the time to encourage small and undiversified banks to crop up. Together, these factors created an environment where panic could spread quickly. The high farm debt came partly from increased prices of agricultural goods during the first world war, which led to increased borrowing by farmers trying to increase their production by investing in machinery and land. The reduced prices for farm commodities after the war made it hard for these farmers to maintain their loan payments.

Some economists argue that the Federal Reserve did not do much to try and deal with the banking panics. In their book written in 1963, Milton Friedman and Anna Schwartz argue that the death of the Federal Reserve Bank governor in 1914 was a significant cause of the inaction. Benjamin Strong, the governor, had been a strong leader who understood the kind of influence a central bank has in limiting panics. His death created a power vacuum that allowed less sensible leaders to avoid any effective intervention. Expectedly, the panics increased the amount of money people chose to hold relative to their bank deposits. This increase was a significant reason why countries worldwide were experiencing a decline in money supply. It didn't help that during the Great Depression, the Federal Reserve, owing to the gold standard, deliberately contracted the supply of money and increased interest rates.

THE DISASTROUS EFFECTS OF THE GREAT DEPRESSION

Almost everyone was affected by the Great Depression, but they were not all affected to the same degree. Many people lost their jobs, and even those who did not lose their jobs experienced adverse effects from low levels of economic growth and business investment. For example, if you lived in a neighborhood and your neighborhood bank failed, getting a small business loan or a mortgage became harder. This was happening all over the globe, making the Great Depression a time of terrible suffering. There were so many contradictions that you did not need to be an economist to know something was wrong. Imagine seeing a child with rickets, shaking as if they have palsy because they have no access to protein or milk. Then, imagine a company pouring milk into the gutters.

During that period, the people plowing cotton fields had nothing to wear. It was hungry people who were killing pigs during emergency livestock reductions. It is hard to imagine a crazier system in the world. One of the surprising things was that people blamed themselves instead of blaming the system. They felt that the fault had to be their own, somehow; '. . . if we had not bought that car or radio.' The fundamentalists did not help matters—they would tell people that their suffering resulted from their sins. And people believed that God was punishing them. Their children were starved because of their sins.

The independent people, who imagined themselves as the mistresses and masters of their fate, suddenly had to depend on others.

One historian says that the Great Depression was the first time he saw the other side of the tracks, the people who were not like him. He saw the world like it was, and it shook him. According to this historian, the depression affected people in two significant ways. The majority of people started believing that money was the most important thing in the world. All you needed to do was get yours and secure it for yours and your children's children. Nothing else mattered. The second group of people, the smaller group, came out of the depression, blaming the system. They felt the system was lousy and knew they had to change it. They taught their kids to want to change the system.

Regardless of where you fell in that historian's divide, you felt the immediate and long-term effects of the Great Depression. The stock market crash, for example, had its effects ripple throughout the financial community, causing banks to fail. It slowed down the growth of economies, increased unemployment rates, and lowered business activity. It is said that more than 33% of all banks in the US failed. Unemployment rose to 25%, and there were more homeless people than there had ever been before. Housing prices went up, deflation soared, and international trade collapsed. It would take more than 20 years for the stock market to recover.

In the first five years of the depression, the world economy shrank by 50%. In the US, the economic output was $105 billion in 1929—the equivalent of over a trillion today. The economy began shrinking, and by the end of the year, the economy had shrunk by 8.5%. GDP growth reduced by 6.4% in 1931; by 1933, the country only produced half of what it did in 1929. Part of the economic contraction was owed to deflation. The Bureau of Labor Statistics said inflation had fallen by 25%, sending many farms into bankruptcy.

The Great Depression also affected farmers who could no longer afford to service their loans or hold out for long. To make things worse, agricultural product prices dropped, so many farmers lost their properties to banks, left in search of work, and became homeless. Thousands of people with no money congregated in cardboard shacks and tried to make it through another day. The depression was so severe that many people in the US thought it to be the end of the American Dream—an ideal that guaranteed rights to a person's vision of happiness. It changed that dream to include the right to material benefits. By 1930, more than 25% of the US workforce was unemployed, making it the highest-ever unemployment rate in the country. One thing came out of the Great Depression that was a ray of hope—the New Deal programs that were set up as safeguards to reduce the likelihood that the depression could happen again. The programs helped to reduce unemployment in the four years after 1931.

As countries worldwide saw their economies worsen, they started creating trade barriers to protect their local industries. The US, for example, set up the Smoot-Hawley tariffs in an effort to protect jobs. Other countries retaliated by creating trading blocs based on trade currencies and national alliances. World trade was reduced by 66%. Imports from Europe declined, dropping from $1.3 billion to $390 million. Exports dropped from $2.3 billion to $784 million. The prices of durable commodities fell by 30%. Deflation helped some consumers whose income had been reduced, but many could not afford basic necessities. Businesses, homeowners, and farmers were hurt because they still had to pay high mortgage rates.

Four years after the stock market crash, at the lowest points of the Great Depression, many in the US workforce were unemployed, and those lucky enough to still be employed saw their wages cut. Even the professionals belonging to the upper middle class, like lawyers and doctors, had their incomes drop by more than 40%. Families who had previously been financially secure suddenly had to grapple with financial instability. The average US family lived by the motto: 'Use it up completely, make do, or do without.' Some people tried to keep up appearances, but most had to adapt to new economic circumstances. Households became frugal in their daily lives. They started keeping kitchen gardens and patching up their clothes.

Not just in the US but all over the globe, thrift gardens and potlucks became the norm. Radio shows of the time and women's magazines were about teaching people how to be homemakers in a depression. Women learned how to stretch their food budgets. Churches organized potlucks as a way to share food and provide cheap entertainment. Families started striving for self-sufficiency by planting as many herbs and vegetables as they could. Cities and towns allowed vacant lots to be made into thrift gardens. England, Austria, Germany, and Poland, the most affected countries, saw their industrial outputs decrease by more than 40%. Trade between European countries collapsed, and by 1932, European trade had fallen to 30% of its original level. Banking currencies in Europe were on the brink of collapse.

By the end of the decade, Europe was starting to see a semblance of recovery, but it was neither sustained nor complete. If war preparations (for the Second World War) had not created investment and demand, the world would probably have entered another depression after 1937. All levels of European society were affected. As a result, domestic politics became turbulent. Politicians failed to introduce policies to deal with the crisis and lost to extremist parties to the left and the right of the political spectrum. In 1931, Britain tried to deal with this trend by creating a national government made up of members from all parties to try and build national unity. Similar developments were happening in the Netherlands, Belgium, and France.

Relations between countries did not escape unscathed during the Great Depression. The severity of the crisis made it such that countries were only interested in protecting their national interests. Toward the end of 1932, every European country had created or enhanced quota systems and tariffs that prevented imports from affecting domestic agriculture and industry. The world was now divided into competing blocs, which had significant implications for international peace. For Italy and Germany, economic nationalism seemed to be the first step on the road to creating new empires: by 1935, it became clear that their nationalism was not confined to economics as Hitler and Mussolini started asserting territorial claims in Eastern Europe, Africa, and the Mediterranean. By then, it was clear that the depression had undermined the ability of some countries to resist demands by these two leaders. Thanks to their economic troubles, France and Britain felt weak and diplomatic cooperation did not seem feasible in an environment of intense economic competition.

It makes sense to complete this section on the impacts of the Great Depression by considering how it affected banking as an industry. One year into the Great Depression, over a third of the banks in the world had failed. By 1933, more than 70% of all banks worldwide had failed, resulting in significant losses for depositors. In the US, for example, people were shocked to realize that their banks had used their deposits to invest in the stock market. They rushed to get their money before it was too late and ran those banks out of business. In the meantime, the stock market lost 90% of its value in three years. People lost confidence in Wall Street. Individual investors, banks, and businesses were wiped out. Even people who had made no investments lost money because the banks had lent it from their savings accounts.

HOW CENTRAL BANKS RESPONDED TO THE CRISIS

Economic historians have characterized the Great Depression as a disaster because of its consequences, how long it took, and its depth. It lasted a decade, beginning in 1929 and ending when the Second World War began. It was characterized by financial crises, banking panics, and the stock market crash. It hit rock bottom in 1933 when the commercial banking system collapsed, and the US president declared a national banking holiday. Then, sweeping reforms of the financial system were implemented, which led to economic recovery and, eventually, the return to full employment and output during the Second World War.

There are some things to note to understand how the central banks saved the world during this period. First, the actions of central banks were not always saintly. When the depression started, the Federal Reserve had a decision-making structure that was decentralized and ineffective. Every district had its governor, who created policies for his district. While some decisions needed the approval of Federal Reserve Boards, the boards did not have the authority or the necessary tools to act alone. It was also struggling to coordinate policies across districts. The governors and the boards understood how necessary coordination was and frequently corresponded about essential issues. They even set up programs and procedures, like the Open Market Investment Committee, to make cooperation institutionalized. In the few instances that these efforts created consensus, monetary policy was fast and effective. However, whenever governors disagreed, districts pursued independent and sometimes contradictory actions.

As it was, the governors disagreed on many issues because experts could not agree on the best course of action, even regarding the conceptual framework for creating the best policy. Information about the state of the economy became available with long lags, which were all variable. Within the Federal Reserve, among policymakers, and in the business community, the perceptions of events differed, meaning that the advocacy for solutions was different. Researchers were divided when it came to these issues. Eventually, a consensus emerged, but not before the divisions had ravaging effects. The leaders of the

Federal Reserve created policies that they believed to serve the interests of the public, but unintentionally, some of their choices hurt the economy. Other policies which could have helped were not adopted early enough.

An example of the Fed's actions hurting the economy would be the former decision of the Fed to raise interest rates in 1928 and 1929. The Fed tried to reduce speculation in the securities markets, but this action slowed the economy. Since the international gold standard connected those interest rates and monetary policies in other countries, the Fed's actions affected the globe. It would repeat the mistake in 1931. Another example of its failure to act was when it did not lend to banks as a lender of last resort during the banking panics, an action that ended with the declaration of a banking holiday.

One of the main reasons the Federal Reserve was created was to be a lender of last resort. Why did it not perform this fundamental task? History shows that the leaders could not agree on the best response to the financial crisis. Some governors thought that during financial panics, central banks needed to loan money to solvent financial institutions beset by panic. Others thought that central banks should give more money to commercial banks during economic expansions and less in times of crisis. By this doctrine, they would recommend that central banks contract credit. The latter doctrine did not describe how to respond to banking panics definitively, but those who believed it thought such panics were a symptom of a contraction. A few governors also thought central banks needed to stand aside during financial panics and let the troubled financial institutions fail. The weak would be pruned, resulting in a healthier economic system.

These intellectual tensions within the Federal Reserve's leadership made the decision-making structure very ineffective and sometimes impossible, which halted the action of the Fed for a while. Federal Reserve leaders also differed in opinion regarding how much help should be given to financial institutions that did not belong to the Federal Reserve System. According to some leaders, support could only be extended to commercial banks that belonged to the Federal Reserve System. Others believed that member banks should get substantial help, enough to help their customers even if they did not belong to the Federal Reserve System. Even so, there was no consensus on the legality of this assistance. Only a few people thought that the Federal Reserve should help commercial banks that were outside its reach.

These differences contributed to one of the Federal Reserve's most influential sins of omission: failing to step in when the money supply was declining. From 1930 to 1933, the money supply was reduced by close to 30%. The reduction caused a concurrent decrease in the average prices and caused an increase in debt burdens, lowered consumption, distorted economic decision-making, and increased unemployment. It also forced people and banks into bankruptcy. The Federal Reserve could have prevented the collapse of the banking system or counteracted it by expanding the monetary base, but it did not for many reasons. For starters, the economic collapse was not only unprecedented, but it was also unforeseen. Decision-makers did not have the mechanisms to determine what went wrong or the authority to act to restore the economy. Some misinterpreted signals about the economy, like the nominal interest rate, because they adhered to the wrong doctrine.

On several occasions, the Federal Reserve created policies resulting from the depression. In 1931, it started expanding the monetary base, but the expansion was insufficient to offset the effects of deflation during the banking crises. In 1932, Congress gave the Federal Reserve the necessary authority and began aggressively expanding the monetary base. Initially, This policy was adequate, but the Federal Reserve changed course shortly after. As a result, some international and political shocks hit the economy. At that point, the Federal Reserve's actions seemed to be a little too late. Despite these flaws of the Federal Reserve, though, the central bank did save the world.

Congress first reformed the Federal Reserve and the whole financial system. Under the administration of Hoover, they instituted congressional reforms that created the Reconstruction Finance Corporation and Banking Act. When Roosevelt became president, other reforms followed, including the 1933 Banking Act, the Gold Reserve Act of 1934, etc. These legislations shifted the responsibilities of the Federal Reserve and made it possible for central banks to save the world. The reforms turned the Federal Reserve into a modern central bank. They created an intellectual framework that helped, even though the underlying economic policy took longer to take shape.

It's worth noting that bank panics would typically be resolved in weeks before the Fed existed. Large private financial institutions would lend money to the strongest smaller institutions to maintain the system's integrity. This kind of scenario happened during a panic in 1907. When the New York Stock Exchange was spiraling downward, a bank contacted the investment banker J.P. Morgan and requested help. Morgan rallied denizens from Wall Street and moved a lot of money to banks that did not have the funds they needed. Ironically, that panic led the government to create the Federal Reserve so that banks would not have to rely on financiers like J.P. Morgan.

After Black Thursday, the leaders of some New York banks tried to instill confidence in the public by prominently buying large blocks of stocks at prices way above market. These actions temporarily caused a rally, but they did not last. The panicked selloffs continued. After the 1929 crash, the Fed was big enough to prop up the financial system in the US, but it did not inject that cash in good time. Instead, it watched the money supply reduce and let thousands of banks fail. Banking laws of the time made it very hard for institutions to grow and become diverse enough to survive a significant deposit withdrawal. The bottom line was that the Fed was afraid to bail out careless banks, imagining such an action would encourage future fiscal irresponsibility.

Besides this, the actions of central bank leaders prevented the depression from being worse than it was. Hebert Hoover was among the first central bank leaders to take action by propping up prices after the crash happened, even though some people thought he did not act. Between 1930 and 1932, he increased federal spending by more than 40%, which engaged different public works programs like the Reconstruction Finance Corporation (RFC). He had taxes set aside to pay for new programs and instituted an immigration ban which kept low-skilled workers from flooding the labor market.

Hoover was mainly concerned about reduced wages following the depression. He figured that prices needed to remain high to ensure people in all industries were paid. For that to happen, consumers needed to pay more. However, the crash badly affected the public, leaving people without resources to spend on goods and services. Companies were unwilling to buy overpriced goods. Hoover's RFC became the government's general-purpose institution, helping three classes of banks—closed banks, banks that had been restricted, and unrestricted banks, which needed to be more liquid, solvent, or both.

By March 1933, the RFC lent more than $80 million to closed bank liquidators. That amount increased more than ten times by 1937. The loans made money available to depositors quickly, which helped liquidators to realize more on assets by disposing of them in an orderly way. The result? A decrease in the downward pressure of bank assets on market prices. The RFC also offered smaller volumes of loans which helped their recovery by increasing bank solvency. The RFC achieved this by subscribing to preferred stock or equity claims against these banks. Essentially, it was creating a system of insuring bank deposits. To prop prices up, Hoover also had to use legislation to choke cheaper foreign competition out. He first signed the Smoot-Hawley Tariff Act to protect agriculture, but it soon became a multi-industry tariff, placing duties on over 880 foreign products. More than 30 countries were affected, and they retaliated.

President Roosevelt came in with the New Deal, a series of domestic acts and programs meant to bolster business, lower unemployment, and keep the public safe. The New Deal was based on the fact that the government should stimulate the economy. It created enormous goals for maintaining infrastructure on a national level and keeping wages healthy. The government was to do this by controlling production, wages, and prices. Some economists think Roosevelt's work was an advancement of Hoover's—only on a large scale. Roosevelt maintained a focus on minimum wages and price supports and removed the gold standard, forbidding people from hoarding bullion and gold coins. He banned businesses that had monopolistic practices and instituted many public works programs. His administration used central banks to pay ranchers and farmers so that they could cut back on production. One of the most brutal facts of the time was the destruction of excess crops, even though thousands of Americans did not have access to food.

Between 1933 and 1940, federal taxes were tripled to pay for the New Deal initiatives, and programs like Social Security were started. The tax increases included personal income taxes, excess profits, excise taxes, etc. The New Deal created many measurable results. It initiated reform and stabilized the financial system, boosting the public's confidence. The bank holiday was followed by a program for constructing roads, tunnels, bridges, and dams, which all opened up work programs and employed thousands. Even though the economy was recovering, the recovery was still weak, so the New Deal policies could not be said to have unequivocally pulled the country out of the Great Depression. It seems as if the Great Depression ended suddenly around 1942 when the US entered the Second World War. Over 16 million Americans fought in the Armed Services. The war opened up international trading channels and reversed wage and price controls. A few years later, the stock market broke into a bull run.

THE LEGACY OF CENTRAL BANK INTERVENTION

The 1933 Banking Act led to the establishment of the FDIC (Federal Deposit Insurance Corporation), whose primary role was to offer a supplementary stabilizing device for banks. The FDIC prevents the occurrence of banking panics by providing insurance for deposits of more than 60 million Americans. The act offered two insurance plans—a temporary plan that was effected in 1934 and a permanent one that followed after the bugs of the temporary plan were worked out. It became mandatory for all banks to join the FDIC. There were requirements for nonmember banks to enter. Most chose to be part of the FDIC because people believe more in insured banks. As a result, the insured banks got more return of currency than uninsured banks.

FDR changed the gold standard to protect the dollar's value, which set a precedent for President Nixon to end it entirely later in 1973. Not only that, but the New Deal programs built many of the landmarks we see today, including the Chrysler Building, the Dealey Plaza in Dallas, and the Rockefeller Center. It was responsible for bridges such as the Golden Gate Bridge and the Triborough Bridge in New York and the Lincoln Tunnel, Hoover Dam, and the LaGuardia Airport, among others. Three entire towns developed due to the intervention of the central banks, including Greenhills, Greendale, and Greenbelt.

New Deal legislation ushered the country into a new period of government regulations with an underlying concept of a free enterprise system with federal oversight. Today, the separation between commercial and investment banking would not exist without the involvement of the central banks during the Great Depression. The FDIC, which provides oversight to banks and protects consumers, would also be nonexistent, and so would the Securities and Exchange Commission (SEC), which oversees the stock market and protects investors from fraud. Perhaps, though, the most significant legacy of the involvement of central banks is the change in the view of the responsibilities governments have toward their people in addressing social and economic problems.

3

FROM THE GOLD STANDARD TO DIGITAL CURRENCIES:

THE MODERN EVOLUTION OF CENTRAL BANKING

> *"Money is a tool to transfer purchasing power from the present to the future."*
>
> — **MILTON FRIEDMAN**

Many people have heard of the gold standard, but few understand it. It was a system where gold and claims to gold were considered money. If you lived in a nation operating under the gold standard, your currency could be changed to a specific amount of gold depending on the international value of your currency. Like any other international monetary standard, the gold standard decreased the transaction costs of trade between countries. In the early 20th century, many industrialized countries used the gold standard. Central banks backed by the state ran the standard internationally. However, as will be discussed later in this chapter, the gold standard collapsed after the end of the Great Depression.

Some historians say that in the final decades of the international gold standard, the volatile prices experienced resulted from mismanagement. They argue that the Great Depression and the First World War triggered the instability. When the First World War started, the standard was no longer functioning. Countries like the UK, Germany, and France stopped using it, choosing to spend their gold and printing money to use as capital during the war. Even the US, which maintained the gold standard for a little longer, disallowed gold exportation during the war. This created several problems.

First, when countries started printing money not backed by gold, they devalued the market exchange rates for their currencies. Later, they failed dismally when they tried to re-establish the old prewar exchange rates. Second, doing away with the gold standard left the international gold price weaker, increasing price levels. As countries tried to re-establish the gold standard after the war, markets had to deal with the opposite problem—prices were collapsing. In his book *The Midas Paradox,* the economist Scott Sumner says that the gold standard had a more considerable effect on policymaker decisions than the size of the economy. Any disturbance in the market, such as the discovery of gold in countries that were not using the gold standard or even the private hoarding of gold, could affect the economic conditions in a country. According to

Sumner, it would be nearly impossible to understand the Great Depression without focusing on the dysfunction within the international gold market.

After the 1929 stock market crash, the decline in prices dramatically increased the demand for gold within central banks. As a result, central banks started growing the amounts of gold they had in their reserves. As the value of gold rose, the prices started falling. This stressed the banking system in new and unprecedented ways. The banking panics only reinforced a growing crisis, increasing the demand for gold rather than banknotes. The gold standard started collapsing in the US and other countries where central banks did a monetary intervention. Erratic policy within central banks made price fluctuations tremendous in the 1930s. Eventually, developed countries decided to abandon the gold standard. Some economists argue that the gold standard fell because of poor management by central banks and not because gold or commodity money was the problem.

Whatever the case, in the gold standard era, any paper money had its value linked to gold. Countries would agree on the amount of gold equivalent to a given currency. For example, if the US set the price of an ounce of gold at $500, the dollar would be valued at 1/500th of an ounce of gold. Today, no government in the world uses the gold standard. Britain abandoned it in 1931; the US began efforts to leave it in 1933 and finally abandoned it in 1973. The gold standard got replaced by fiat money—a term for currency based on an order given by the government, or fiat, that the currency must be accepted as a mode of payment. The dollar, for example, is fiat money in the US.

The gold standard was appealing because it removed control of the issuing of money from the hands of people. The physical quantity of gold was the limit to the issuance, so society could live by simple rules and avoid inflation. Today, the goal of monetary policy is not just to prevent inflation but also deflation, like what was experienced during the Great Depression. It is to promote a stable environment where everyone can be employed. To understand how our world came to that conclusion, we must consider how the gold standard came to be.

THE HISTORY OF THE GOLD STANDARD

Under the gold standard, the value of different currencies was based on gold, but in a fiat system, the value of a currency is not based on physical commodities. It can change dynamically against other currencies as it trades on foreign exchange markets. Derived from the Latin word translated to an arbitrary decree, the term 'fiat' stays true to its name. Fiat currency is based on the fact that it is defined as legal tender because governments decree it. In the years preceding the First World War, since international trade was based on the gold standard, trade was settled using physical gold. This meant that countries that had trade surpluses accumulated gold as payment. Conversely, those with deficits saw their reserves decline as they paid for imports with gold.

Speaking on the gold standard, President Herbert Hoover would later say that 'we have gold because we are not able to trust governments.' Perhaps without meaning it, the president's statement foreshadowed one of the most draconian events in the financial history of the US—the Emergency Banking Act—where every citizen was forced to convert all their bullion, gold coins, and certificates into the US dollar. Admittedly, the legislation managed to stop the outflow of gold during the Great Depression, but it did not change the conviction of some people who are forever confident that gold is a stable source of wealth—gold bugs.

As it is, gold has a unique history that no other asset class enjoys in its ability to influence its demand and supply. Gold bugs still believe that the age of gold is not over, but to understand the past that gold rules, one must also look at the fall of the gold standard to understand the future of gold. For 5,000 years, gold's combination of density, malleability, scarcity, and lister has captivated human beings like no other metal. One historian, talking about the power of gold, said of the metal that it is so dense that a ton of it can be packed into a cubic foot. Imagine that.

The beginning of humankind's obsession with gold started in temples. Gold was only used for worship at the time. Ancient sacred sites had altars or temple equipment made entirely of gold or lined with gold. With time, the use of gold evolved, so today, gold is most prevalent in jewelry manufacture. Around 700 BC, gold was made into coins for the first time in history, enhancing the metal's usability as money. Before this, the gold had to be weighed and checked for purity before any trade could be performed. Of course, gold coins were not a perfect solution. For centuries, it was common practice for people to clip irregular coins to get enough gold to melt it into bullion.

In 1696, the Houses of Parliament passed an act to remedy this problem in England. After much debate, the government melted down and reissued all the country's silver coins, plates, and bullion according to an Elizabethan standard. The parliament issued a deadline for depositing old coins. The great recoinage was already happening when Newton arrived at the mint. The new coins would be produced using new techniques tested earlier in the century. They would have intricate stamps and milled ages, making the coins uniform and hard to counterfeit. Workers and subcontractors were put under oath. However, the process met with many technical difficulties and accusations of corruption and mismanagement. It was Newton who helped to improve the security and efficiency of the recoinage.

It is said that Newton ran experiments to do this. He wanted to reduce waste and profiteering by the subcontractors, mint employees, and financiers. He was responsible for the provisional mints set up in Bristol, Chester, and other strategic locations. The locations were chosen for their position as hubs for international trade. This change happening in Europe rippled to the rest of the world. It introduced technology that automated the process of coin production and brought an end to clipping. Since the supply of gold could not always rely on additional supplies from the earth, it expanded only through debasement, pillage, trade, and deflation.

The first American gold rush happened in the 15th century. Spain had plundered the New World and raised Europe's gold supply five times in the 16th century. The subsequent gold rushes in Australia, the Americas, and South Africa happened in the 19th century. This was the era pre the gold standard. Notably, Europe first introduced paper money in the 16th century using debt instruments given to private parties. Bullion and gold coins remained the dominant monetary system in Europe until the 18th century when things started to change, and paper money started to dominate. The struggle between gold and paper money would eventually create the gold standard.

THE GOLD STANDARD RISES

In the gold standard, gold backs the value of money. Between the Great Recoinage and 1812, the development and institutionalization of the gold standard started as paper money introduced some problems. In 1789, the US Constitution gave Congress the right to make money and the power to regulate how it was valued. The idea was to create a united national currency that would help to standardize the monetary system. At the time, silver coins were more widely circulated. This meant that silver was more in abundance than gold. So, in 1792, the world adopted a bimetallic standard. The official parity ratio of silver to gold was 15:1, accurately reflecting the time's market ratio. However, after 1793, the value of silver went on a steady decline, pushing gold out of circulation. This problem continued for a while, creating animosity between people and institutions until 1834.

Officially, the price of gold stayed consistent at $19.75 per ounce. It was raised in 1834 to get to $20.67. To reconcile the new value of gold, Congress passed the 1834 Coinage Act. According to the new regulation, the value and weight of gold would be synchronized with the marketplace and the value of silver. As a result, the parity ratio of gold to silver changed to 1:16. At the time, hard money enthusiasts were not happy about the move. They advocated for a ratio appropriate for reintroducing gold back into circulation, not pushing silver out. They wanted the paper notes issued by the central bank to be pushed out instead. The 16:1 ratio blatantly overvalued gold, putting the US on a de facto gold standard.

In 1821, England officially became the first country to take up the gold standard. The century saw a dramatic increase in production and global trade, which brought significant gold discoveries in England and helped keep the gold standard intact. All trade imbalances between countries would be settled in gold, so governments had strong incentives to hoard gold for difficult times. Some of those stockpiles exist even today.

It took another 50 years since England adopted the gold standard for the international gold standard to become formalized. It emerged in 1871 after Germany adopted it. By 1900, most developed nations were now connected by the gold standard. Ironically, the US was among the last nations to join the standard. The country's strong silver lobby stood in the way of gold being the only monetary standard. Between 1871 and 1914, the gold standard was at its peak. At this time, most countries enjoyed a nearly ideal political climate, including India, Canada, Australia, and New Zealand. The gold standard was working well.

THE GOLD STANDARD FALLS

However, things changed in 1914 when the Great War broke out. During the First World War, political alliances changed constantly. Countries were heavily in debt, and government finances deteriorated. The gold standard was still the monetary system of the period, but it seemed to be in limbo during the war. Some economists said this proves that the standard could not hold in the bad times. This created a lack of confidence in the gold standard, which only made the economic difficulties experienced even worse. It soon became clear that the world needed something more flexible to serve as the base for the global economy.

Concurrently, there was a pervasive public desire to return to the gold standard's idyllic years in many nations. Bear in mind that the supply of gold was continually falling behind the growth of the global economy. At this time, the US dollar and the British pound sterling became the international reserve currencies. Smaller nations started holding more of the pound and the dollar than they did gold. The result was that the more prominent nations had a consolidated supply of gold. The 1929 stock market crash soon followed, and closely behind it were other tragedies. For example, the French franc and the pound became misaligned with other currencies, repatriations and war debts ravaged Germany, commodity prices collapsed, and banks could no longer hold their own.

Most countries tried protecting their gold stock by increasing interest rates to draw investors and keep their deposits untouched instead of converting them to gold. The increased interest rates hurt the global economy. Great Britain was the first to suspend the gold standard in 1931. Francc and the US were left with large reserves of gold. In 1934, the US revalued gold to $35 per ounce and increased the amount of paper money it took to secure an ounce of gold in an effort to improve the economy. The dollar was dramatically devalued because other countries could convert their gold holdings into US dollars. The increased price of gold raised the conversion of gold to US dollars, effectively allowing the country to corner the market. By 1939, the production of gold had soared so much that there was enough of it in the world to replace all the global currencies in circulation.

As the Second World War ended, the leading Western powers met to create the Bretton Woods Agreement. The agreement would serve as a framework for the global currency market. Within the system, all currencies would be valued in relation to the US dollar, so the dollar became the dominant reserve currency. In turn, the dollar could be converted to gold at a $35 per ounce fixed rate. The global financial system was still operating based on the gold standard, even though this time, it was indirect. Over time, the agreement created an interesting relationship between the US dollar and gold. In the long run, if the dollar declines, it means gold prices rise. On a short-term level, this is not always true. At best, the relationship is tenuous.

At the end of the Second World War, the US had 75% of all the monetary gold in the world, and the dollar was the only currency directly backed by gold. However, as the world started rebuilding, gold reserves in the US dropped as money flowed to nations torn by war, and the US experienced high import demand. The inflation of the late 1960s ended up being the final straw that ended the Bretton Woods system and the Gold Standard. Notably, in 1968, the Gold Pool, which included some European nations and the US, stopped selling gold on the London market and allowed it to determine the price of gold freely. Three years later, only central banks were allowed to trade with the US at $35 per ounce. The gold pool meant that the exchange rates of currencies could be set at a par level and adjusted with economic conditions. This removed pressure from member nations so that they could appreciate their currencies and have export-led growth strategies.

There was an unforeseen challenge, though. Foreign nations were becoming increasingly competitive, and debt was being issued to pay for the Vietnam War and social programs. These factors started weighing on America's money. Soon enough, the surplus turned into a deficit, and in 1959, there were fears that foreign nations would begin redeeming their assets (primarily dollar-denominated) for gold. The problem was so infectious that Senator John F. Kennedy ran his campaign on a promise that if elected, he would not devalue the dollar. In 1968, the Gold Pool collapsed because member nations were unwilling to cooperate to maintain the market price at the US gold rate. The years that followed saw countries like the Netherlands and Belgium cash in dollars for gold. France and Germany had similar intentions.

In 1971, Britain forced Nixon's hand by requesting their payments be made in gold, officially closing the era of the gold standard. By 1976, it became globally accepted that the dollar would not be defined by gold. Later in 1971, after Britain forced Nixon's hand, he severed the direct link between the US dollar and gold. This decision meant that the international currency market, which by then was heavily reliant on the dollar (after the Bretton Woods agreement), lost its official connection to gold. By extension, the US dollar and the global financial system it sustained entered an era of fiat money.

While gold has fascinated people for over 5,000 years, it was not always the basis for our monetary system. The international gold standard existed for less than 50 years before 1914. A lesser form of the standard remained until 1971, but its death began centuries before when paper money was introduced. Paper money is a more flexible tool suited for our complex financial world. Today, how gold is priced depends on demand and supply. It is no longer a standard, but it serves a significant function—it is a major financial asset for central banks and countries. Banks use it to hedge against the loans they make to their governments. It is used as a marker of economic health.

Perhaps, under the free market system, gold would be seen as a currency in the same class as the US dollar, yen, or euro. It has had a long-standing relationship with the dollar and may have an inverse relationship over time. It is common to hear people talking about creating another gold standard, but that system has flaws. Maybe seeing gold as a currency and treating it that way in trade may mitigate the risks. Whatever the case, we can agree that gold is forward-looking. When there is an impending disaster, as long as you do not wait for the price of gold to reflect a slumping economy, having it will be an advantage.

THE EMERGENCE OF MODERN CENTRAL BANKING

The earliest banks arose to solve a fundamental issue for a monetary economy—how to keep money safe and how to make payments. The goal of a monetary system is to offer an instrument that facilitates instantaneous, verifiable, and ubiquitous transfers of an asset at zero cost. That's how coins and banknotes came to be, and later on, credit cards and, today, digital money. Traditionally, coins issued by central banks were precious metals. Central banks had to determine how to get the metals accepted by face value, not by weight. The following money innovation was the issuing of notes. Here, the problem to overcome was the issue of the cost of precious metals. And in Italy, commercial banks started issuing receipts that revolutionized the world of money.

Early central banks, like the Bank of Amsterdam, were public-private businesses. They could use their balance sheets to create efficient payment systems, and their ledger money could be swapped or used as an implicit guarantee of backed-up value. I bring up these facts because they are still the principles that underpin modern central banks. The Bank of England is considered to be the first-ever modern central bank. It served as a benchmark for central banks that followed. Later, central banks had a monopoly over currency and began to work to correct their deficiencies (the Great Recoinage). Modern central banks have evolved from their early beginnings to the present day, with each iteration looking to serve or correct for a specific public need.

War financing was a key driver for modern central banks toward the end of the 17th and early 18th centuries. Central banks played a crucial role in raising money through debt issuance. These were the chief goals of the Riksbank and the Bank of England. Since then, central banks have been involved in managing government debt. Its role in public finance was enhanced with the introduction of fiat money, acting as an effective way to fund fiscal deficits. Throughout history, you will see that fiscal dominance has been a recurring theme. Even so, monetary and fiscal authorities have always been intertwined, with the currency being backed by fiscal power.

While the early central banks existed to fund government debt, they were also private businesses that carried out other banking activities. Since they carried deposits for different banks, they became the banker's bank, enjoying extensive networks and large reserves. This is true even today. Even more so, modern central banks play a significant role in maintaining financial stability, drawing from the model of banks in Britain that served as lenders of last resort. These banks follow Bagehot's rule that in the face of a banking panic, they are to lend to banks freely as long as they provide sound collateral. When faced with a speculative attack, the banks must also lend freely but at higher rates. Recently, central banks have expanded to act as a lender of last resort, even to nonbank financial intermediaries.

Most proto-central banks operated under the gold standard, whose main rule was to convert notes to gold at a fixed price. The pioneering Bank of England learned to keep the economy stable and maintain gold convertibility in the face of internal and external shocks. It was particularly successful because of its credibility. Together with other central banks, it perfected discount rates as a vital policy tool and, later on, open market operations. Modern central banks are adding tools to these but under the same principle of keeping the value of money stable.

Central banks learned to provide macro stability and create a countercyclical monetary policy during and after the Second World War. It was a slow and painful process to learn these lessons, especially after the policy disasters of the Great Depression, but the lessons have now shaped modern central banks. Other innovations of the time include keeping the central bank independent of the government and using Taylor-type instrument rules as a guide. Because of these historical events, the modern central bank has two main functions—macroeconomic and microeconomic.

On a macroeconomic level, the modern central bank aims for price stability. Its job is to regulate inflation by controlling the money supply and monetary policy. It runs open market transactions that add cash liquidity or absorb extra cash, directly influencing inflation. When central banks are trying to increase the amount of money in circulation and lower the interest rates on borrowing, they will often buy government bills, bonds, or other notes issued by the government. Still, they must be careful because this buying can cause more inflation. Central banks sell government bonds to absorb money and reduce inflation, increasing interest rates and discouraging borrowing.

On a microeconomic level, modern central banks are lenders of last resort. A commercial bank gives money to clients based on who will be most profitable for them, given the least risk. It can borrow additional funds from central banks if it does not have enough liquidity to serve its clients (commercial banks do not usually have reserves to meet market needs). This makes the system stable, objectively speaking. In addition, central banks are not allowed to favor any one commercial bank. They hold commercial-bank reserves based on the commercial bank's deposits. And that's why they lay liquidity and solvency requirements on commercial banks, yet another way to manage the money supply in the market.

Some economists argue that for the open market to function efficiently, discount rates (the rate at which commercial banks borrow from the central bank) need to be sufficiently high to disincentivize banks from perpetual borrowing, but that would disrupt the money supply and the monetary policy of the central banks. By borrowing too much, commercial banks circulate more money in the system. Central banks use the discount rate to manage this by making it unattractive to borrow continually. As it is, developing economies are grappling with issues like transitioning to free market economies. They are still trying to figure out how to control inflation. Some are resorting, as their predecessors did, to the creation of independent central banks.

Unfortunately, many developing countries still deal with civil war and disorder, forcing governments to divert development funds toward resolving these domestic issues. Nonetheless, it is clear from how the modern central bank developed that it needs a stable currency for a market economy to keep steady. It is also clear that modern central banks, whether in emerging or industrial economies, need to be dynamic because there is no one sure way to run an economy. It is also true that it is the job of the modern central bank to oversee the monetary system along with many other responsibilities, including implementing goals for low inflation and currency stability. These roles have grown more critical in the last century, but they evolved in response to other developments in the world.

In most cases, the government or state owns the modern central bank. Still, it is separate from the country's department or Ministry of Finance and makes all decisions independent of political parties. Even though it would often be called the government's bank, it often deals with buying and selling government bills and bonds, with no influence from political decisions. Of course, how the relationship between each bank and its government looks varies from country to country and will keep evolving as time goes by.

HOW DIGITAL CURRENCIES ARE SHAKING UP THE FINANCIAL SYSTEM

When the banking world took up technology from England to make stamped coins less prone to chipping, it responded to a need. When promissory notes and paper money were introduced and finally replaced gold, it was an innovation to make life easier. It appears that today the financial system is on the cusp of another feat of innovation, but how central banks should respond is complex. Digitization has played a significant role in the current change in banking services and functions. In retail, digital currencies could radically impact how banking is structured, with ripple effects for credit intermediation.

Major central banks today are thinking about digital currencies in one way or another. There is even a degree of urgency in much of the work being done. It can be tempting for some banks to park the issue at the bottom of their priority list to return to later. But the potential of digital currencies to disrupt the financial system cannot be ignored. At a minimum, central banks should be working to incorporate some analysis of digital currencies as part of their future planning. Perhaps, more ambitiously, they should create response strategies that integrate existing technology and innovation. Maybe they should also engage in ongoing processes for regulation to make sure they keep up with digitization.

Whatever the case, anyone can agree that the rise of Bitcoin and other cryptocurrencies could affect the practices of central banks and the financial system. One wonders whether paper money will one day become obsolete. Could Bitcoin and other digital currencies replace the euro, the dollar, or the yen? What should central banks do? Should they issue digital currencies? What opportunities do these currencies present, and what dangers do they come with?

A lot of money today is already electronic. True, most countries still use physical currency, except for countries like Sweden, where the use of physical money is shrinking fast. All over the world, consumers routinely run transactions without any physical money changing hands. They use mobile phones and credit cards to make payments. What is more, most of the money that is in central banks exists in electronic form. Strangely, the idea of digital currencies is not entirely novel. When credit cards were introduced into the monetary system, people learned how to manage them, and we lived through it. We may learn how to use digital currencies as well. As it is, most of the money produced by central banks is wholesale and electronic, so paper money is already a tiny fraction of the existing system.

Even so, it is unlikely that cryptocurrencies will replace money backed by the government soon. Bitcoin and other digital currencies may be popular, but they still have a long way to go in earning the trust that the euro, the

Japanese yen, or the US dollar enjoy—central banks back all of these currencies. Although there is reduced confidence in government institutions, most people still go for central bank-backed money, and this may not change soon. Some things digital currencies promised, such as scalability, have not yet been actualized. For example, Bitcoin networks handle a few transactions in a second, but an interbank Visa can take a hundred times more than that. Perhaps that is because investing in digital currencies is lopsided, so a lot of money goes into the mining, and very little goes to the support features.

One of the most underestimated things when we talk about digital currencies is why people use central banks and their payment systems—if one bank sends money to another, that money is not passed through the central bank's payment system. What happens is that one bank gets a claim on the other bank. Bankers do not need to trust each other—that's the job of central banks: to transfer money safely. When a new technology is suddenly introduced in such an arrangement, people expect it would substitute these transactions, but is that expectation realistic? Could digital currencies eradicate centuries of good practices and replicate the trust we enjoy today with fiat currency? Perhaps, or perhaps not. It is clear, though, that digital currencies highlight people's confidence in central banks.

Digital currencies could still revolutionize the financial system. With other innovations within payment systems, digital currencies could increase the speed of cross-border and domestic transactions. They could lower the costs of transactions and eventually improve access to the system for rural and poor households. Undoubtedly, payment systems are getting more and more efficient. In India and China, one can run tiny transactions with street vendors through a decentralized payment system, intermediated through platforms different from traditional banks. That is something that can easily catch on.

New technologies make it easier for everyone to have access to money. Only years ago, it was difficult to imagine sending money from one mobile phone to another in real-time. Who can tell what the future holds with digital currencies? One of the reasons we are seeing some political forces become more powerful is that people do not feel a connection to the economy. When you feel connected to a financial system, you are potent. You believe that reforms in the country would benefit you, so you make them a reality. A big part of the promise of digital currencies is that they will provide more access to more people to the financial system, and that fact alone is transformative.

Of course, these new technologies are not without their troubles. Digital currencies and similar technologies will probably reduce the cost of transactions and lower the price of sharing and acquiring information, which sounds good. Still, they could render financial markets unstable and intensify contagion between markets. They could bring down entire business models, affecting conventional banks and their roles within the financial system. This means that digital currencies could make it hard for central banks to maintain financial stability. Suppose you think about information becoming more accessible because of new technologies. In that case, you can easily assume that financial markets will work better because of it, but academics don't necessarily think that is the case. You could end up with information aggregators who become very powerful in an economy with plenty of information but insufficient processing ability. The result could be situations where you have informational cascades, and some behaviors become worse, not because there is less information but because there is too much unprocessed information.

Over time, many of the inefficiencies of the financial system have eroded, mainly owing to lessons learned during crises. The traditional competitive rents that banks collect may erode as well. It is unclear what the banks of the future will look like. Will they play as influential a role in creating money as they do now? Will commercial banks have a less significant role in finance? What will be the job of central banks when it comes to facilitating and settling payments across financial institutions? How will the implementation of monetary policy change? We must grapple with all these questions because of digital currencies. Just imagine a scenario where different payment systems become decentralized. This means that any official foundation will not anchor the payment systems. What problems could this cause in bad times? What if those decentralized systems start coming apart? This could affect the monetary stability and economies of countries.

In the face of all these questions, one wonders whether central banks should consider issuing their digital currencies as well. Should they allow the public to make electronic deposits at the central bank? Not enough central banks are giving this question as much weight as it deserves, but many are starting to explore it as an option. So far, some central banks, such as Tunisia and Ecuador, have issued their own. Sweden recently issued the e-krona, state-issued digital money. Issuing a digital currency would keep a central bank from losing its market share to other coins like Bitcoin and make it easier for the central bank to charge depositors instead of paying interest in times of an economic downturn. However, an official digital currency could interfere with the role of traditional banks as lenders and intermediaries. It could create significant problems in a financial crisis if depositors remove their money from traditional banks to hold it with the central bank.

A question worth considering is the extent to which it should be possible for the general public to hold a claim to electronic money on the central bank. Should we have a system where only banks could claim e-money from central banks? We know, though, that a digital currency issued by a central bank reduces costs, which benefits everyone. No European central banks have passed negative rates on individual clients yet. A central bank digital currency that bears interest may help deal with some of the constraints of digital currencies. This does not need that physical money to be abolished, but it ceases to be a competitor for large transactions. In such a scenario, the bank could have more control over interest rates. It could reduce those rates in a recession to stabilize economic activity quickly and lower the need for non-conventional measures.

4

UNUSUAL MONETARY POLICIES:

THE GOOD, THE BAD, AND THE UGLY

> *"There are risks and costs to action. But they are far less than the long-range risks of comfortable inaction."*
>
> — **JOHN F. KENNEDY**

The story of Argentina's debt is an excellent place to start. It includes many myths, challenges, and mysteries that lend to a good understanding of unusual monetary practices. In 2005, four years after the default at the end of 2001, the government successfully restructured its debt, implementing a significant 66% reduction. By 2007, just two years later, the credit spreads measured by the Emerging Market Bond Index had substantially decreased from over 6,000 basis points to merely 200 bps, similar to Brazil's levels. This period seemed promising, as the markets appeared to have forgiven Argentina's past mistakes and viewed the country as more creditworthy.

However, there were misconceptions regarding the extent of Argentina's debt reduction in 2005. Contrary to popular belief, the cut was not as substantial as initially perceived. The government included a warrant linked to GDP growth in its offer, allowing bondholders to receive extra payments if the economy grew by more than 3.25% annually. This turned out to be costly for Argentina but beneficial for bondholders. Although investors initially undervalued the warrant during the exchange, they eventually received over 30% of the face value of the defaulted bonds, almost equal to what they received in new bonds. Consequently, the overall debt reduction was less than 40%. This policy decision highlighted the need to design GDP warrants in future sovereign debt restructurings carefully.

One confusing aspect of the Argentine debt restructuring was how they achieved a 78% acceptance rate for an offer that seemed exceedingly harsh at the time. I can think of two explanations. First, when the initial proposal was presented in early 2005 in Doha, its estimated value was $18, implying an 82% reduction. However, by the end of 2005, when the exchange offer was launched, the same proposal was valued at approximately $33, mainly due to the tightening of emerging market sovereign bond spreads. The second reason was that investors felt they had limited alternatives to receive payment if they rejected the offer. This experience revealed an essential lesson: creditors have few effective means to collect funds from a sovereign country unwilling to pay. A government can evade sanctions and evade consequences for an extended period.

Vulture funds, such as Elliott Management, had been litigating against Argentina, attempting to seize assets for over eight years without success until recently. Argentina had no access to international financial markets and resorted to hiding its assets (primarily using the Bank of International Settlements) to avoid attachments. The country's limited borrowing abroad made it challenging for foreign creditors to collect what was owed to them.

Unfortunately, the favorable conditions did not endure for long. Argentina made two significant policy mistakes that ultimately proved highly costly. Firstly, it manipulated the consumer price index to devalue the local currency-indexed debt, a decision many investors viewed as a "technical default." Secondly, as part of a debt reduction policy, Argentina distanced itself from international financial markets and opted not to issue new debt. While this decision aimed to reduce debt service obligations, it meant that Argentina had to rely on international reserves, with no lender of last resort (the IMF was not an option).

This extreme approach to debt reduction became challenging to maintain during years of fiscal deficits or when significant principal payments in foreign currencies were due. A more reasonable approach would have been to set an objective of gradually reducing the debt-to-GDP ratio or adjusting the debt profile by increasing the share of local currency debt. Instead, debt became a political target, and the authorities believed that issuing debt would revive the negative experiences of the past. Consequently, they relied on inflation taxes and depleting international reserves. The reluctance to issue debt left the economy highly vulnerable. While this strategy was feasible during prosperous times when reserves were increasing, it became perilous when reserves began to decline. This marked the start of a challenging period from mid-2007 to 2011, during which Argentine credit spreads widened compared to Brazil and approached levels similar to those of Venezuela.

Argentina faced the grim phase of its debt saga for years as the situation worsened due to several adverse events. The external situation became more complicated in 2011 following Greece's de facto involuntary debt restructuring. Additionally, Argentina's decision to nationalize the oil company YPF without compensating Repsol and the forceful conversion of particular provincial dollar debt issued under domestic legislation into pesos (pesification) added concerns.

Two other issues further complicated the situation. In October 2012, the New York Court of Appeals in the US upheld a lower court ruling that required Argentina to pay $1.3 billion to bondholders of defaulted bonds (mainly vulture funds), either voluntarily or through the attachment of funds allocated for performing bonds. Still pending appeal, this ruling raises the possibility of a new default on Argentina's debt. Unlike the 2001 default, this would not indicate insolvency or lack of funds but rather a refusal to settle with holdout creditors. Following the ruling, Argentine credit spreads surged dramatically, particularly the credit default swap (CDS), reaching 3,500 bps, as the market anticipated a high risk of default on bonds issued under foreign legislation. The impact on bonds issued under domestic legislation was smaller, as the market believed they carried less credit risk.

The second complication was the significant decline in international reserves, dropping from a peak of $52 billion in mid-2011 to a more recent $37 billion. This decline necessitated the implementation of strict foreign exchange controls in 2011, leading to the emergence of a parallel exchange rate. Argentina's sovereign bond spreads skyrocketed in 2013, averaging 60%, adding pressure on reserves and compelling the government to tighten controls further. The simultaneous existence of credit and foreign exchange spreads complicates macroeconomic management, particularly since reversing the decline in international reserves without significant policy changes is challenging. Moreover, the current environment negatively affects investment and growth. This unpleasant phase revives memories of the balance of payments and debt crises. However, the current situation does not involve collapsing commodity prices or widespread emerging market debt crises as in previous occasions.

Argentina was confronted with significant challenges. To some extent, the prospects for improving credit spreads depended on the outcome of the legal battle in New York. Equally important was the approach to debt management. Argentina needed to face the difficulties stemming from its resistance to issuing foreign currency debt, despite the apparent need for dollars to service it. Additionally, the country needed to recognize that the spreads in the parallel exchange market were exacerbating reserve losses, as leakages affected official trade flows, and businesses hesitated to bring financial flows at the official exchange rate due to the high risk of currency depreciation.

The paradox is that Argentina's debt problems occurred in a financially solvent country with reasonably solid macroeconomic fundamentals. As of 2013, the net public sector debt represented only 18% of GDP, and foreign currency debt issued by the private sector (excluding multilateral organizations) was less than 10%. Moreover, a significant portion of the debt is long-term, resulting in relatively small financial requirements in any given year. Additionally, Argentina boasted modest fiscal and current account deficits, 2.5 and 1.0% of GDP, respectively. These figures compared favorably to other Latin American countries such as Brazil, Colombia, and Uruguay.

Hence, the question arises: why did Argentina's credit spreads remain high compared to other emerging markets? The explanation lies in the dual spreads and the persistent decline in reserves, both directly linked to market distrust caused by stringent and unconventional government intervention.

THE UNCONVENTIONAL POLICIES

For decades now, central banks in advanced economies have used policy interest rates as their tool for implementing monetary policy. While responding to the financial crisis of 2008 and the deep recession that resulted from it, many central banks lowered their policy interest rates to almost nonexistent levels. As the world watched economic growth weaken, the interest rates stayed low while others used 'unconventional' monetary policy to drive economic activity. Some of these unconventional measures rose to the forefront again as central banks worldwide responded to the consequences of the global pandemic. This chapter describes the different unconventional policies used worldwide, their risks and benefits, and the controversies surrounding interventions by central banks.

Foundationally, one has to understand what a conventional monetary policy looks like. Typically, traditional policies involve central banks changing a target for interest rates in the short term (policy interest rate) to achieve particular economic objectives. Policy interest rates affect other interest rates in the economy, like the interest rates on savings accounts, business loans, and housing loans. When these interest rates change, it affects the cost of borrowing and rewards for saving, the prices of assets, and the exchange rate. As a result, this influences how people consume or invest and ultimately influences economic activity. By changing interest rates, conventional monetary policy helps the central bank meet its goals for employment, aggregate demand, and inflation. Increased interest rates slow employment and aggregate demand growth and puts negative pressure on inflation. On the other hand, lowering the interest rates stimulates growth in employment and aggregate demand and pushes inflation upward.

In periods of economic crisis or a deep recession, conventional monetary policies come upon a limitation. Nominal interest rates cannot go lower than zero, and bank reserve requirements cannot be lowered so much that the banks risk defaulting. So, once the interest rates are reduced to the lowest possible levels, the economy risks falling into a liquidity trap. In a liquidity trap, people no longer have any incentive to invest. Instead, they hoard money, and this prevents recovery from the crisis.

A liquidity trap can also happen when investors, not just consumers, hoard money rather than invest or spend it even when interest rates have been reduced to near zero, frustrating economic policymakers' efforts to stimulate the economy's growth. The term was first coined by an economist who described it as interest rates falling so low that most people see no need to put their money into debt instruments or bonds. According to the economist, in a liquidity trap, policymakers are left powerless to stimulate economic growth no matter what they try—they cannot increase the supply of money or lower interest rates.

In rare cases, a liquidity trap happens when investors and consumers don't invest their cash because they anticipate a future interest rate increase. As a result, bond prices fall due to a lack of investors purchasing them. The term liquidity trap refers specifically to the fact that policymakers cannot stimulate investment and growth despite lowering interest rates to such low levels. Consumers often save large amounts, believing the economy's future is doomed. If interest rates are already low, then the central bank cannot cut them anymore. If it increases the supply of money, that will create more money for people to hoard. They are firmly bound and driven by their lack of confidence in the future.

It also happens that when consumers hoard money, they also liquidate their investments. They may sell bonds, for example, which lowers their prices and increases yields. Despite yields rising, consumers still have no interest in buying bonds. Their belief in a doomed future is so strong that they prefer to keep cash even though it is not earning much. It is worth noting that in a liquidity trap, banks struggle to attract qualified borrowers for their loan offerings. This is made worse because interest rates are so low that there is zero room for extra incentives to attract suitable candidates. The lack of interest in taking out loans shows up all over the economy, from personal loans to business loans, car loans, and mortgages.

A sure marker of a liquidity trap is seeing near-zero interest rates. With concerns about a country's financial state, near-zero rates affect people's behavior. Bondholders end up selling their bonds at levels that hurt the economy. Meanwhile, consumers resolve to hold their money in low-risk savings. Low interest rates alone do not make a liquidity trap, though—for a situation to qualify as a liquidity trap, people have to be unwilling to keep their bonds, and there has to be a limited supply of willing investors to buy them. Liquidity traps are also characterized by low deflation or inflation. The whole economy becomes resistant to any policy actions by the central bank.

As a result, the bank has to increase the supply of money using open market operations. To do this, the central bank buys securities, usually government bonds, in the open market—an action known as quantitative easing. In a crisis, however, government securities are often bid up due to a flight to safety, limiting its effectiveness as a policy tool. Alternatively, the central bank can purchase other securities in the open market, including corporate bonds and equities.

QUANTITATIVE EASING

Typically, the central bank does not interfere with nongovernment securities markets. These markets are left to operate on their own. However, in times of crisis, the central bank will intervene in these markets. The securities bought during a QE round tend to be debt instruments, including mortgage-backed securities. During quantitative easing, central banks can also purchase debt with different maturities to influence the shape of the yield curve and prop up markets such as housing financed by mortgages. When the central bank buys private company assets such as corporate bonds, that is sometimes referred to as credit easing.

Generally, the Federal Open Market Committee (FOMC) uses three tools to achieve its purpose—open market operations, specifying to banks the reserve requirements, and setting the federal funds rate. In open market operations, the central bank will create money and purchase treasury securities from people, banks, or businesses in the short term. That way, it creates demand and drives their prices up. The demand created ends up injecting money into the system. That money is loaned to people and businesses, putting downward pressure on interest rates and boosting the economy.

Suppose the regular quantitative easing attempts do not work. In that case, the central bank can get even more unconventional in its actions by intervening in equity markets by buying shares in the open market. In the years following the Great Depression, this was one of the actions central banks worldwide took. The central bank can also call on the public to act by letting them know of its intentions to maintain low interest rates for an extended period in an attempt to boost confidence. It can engage in more rounds of quantitative easing until it trickles down to the economy and drives up demand.

Most of the time, central banks will not apply quantitative easing unless open market operations fail. For them, the idea is to do what they must to boost economic activity and introduce money into the system, reducing yields and easing the pressure on some markets by lowering the risk spread. Of course, quantitative easing will affect the central bank's balance sheet and expose it to more risk. It was first used in 2001 when the Bank of Japan responded to the real estate bubble bursting and the deflation that followed. Since then, other central banks, including the Federal Reserve, the European Central Bank, and the Bank of England, have used their versions of quantitative easing.

In 2008, many of these banks turned to quantitative easing to improve the health of their economies. Keep in mind that quantitative easing is different from quantitative tightening. The latter is about removing cash from the economy to manage a situation where it has become overheated. The assets that the Fed bought as part of quantitative easing in 2008 were treasuries and mortgage-backed securities. Between September 2007 and December 2008, the Fed also lowered the rate for federal funds to 0.25% and maintained it there for seven years. It used open market operations to reduce rates for different maturities, explicitly focusing on short-term borrowing.

Between 2008 and 2013, the Fed was also doing quantitative easing by implementing asset purchases on a large scale. At first, it bought over $170 billion in agency debt, triple as much in mortgage-backed securities, and $300 billion in treasury securities. In other rounds, the Fed introduced a maturity extension program that cost more than $660 billion. After close to five years of holding these assets on its balance sheet, the Fed's quantitative easing goals were achieved, so it started the normalization process in 2017.

NEGATIVE INTEREST RATES

If other interventions fail, the central bank can decide to use negative interest rates where rather than paying interest on any money deposited there, depositors have to pay interest to keep their money at the bank. The idea is to make it difficult for people to leave their money in savings and credit accounts. They prefer to invest or spend it rather than get penalized for keeping it. Unfortunately, this policy ends up punishing savers. In a negative interest rate policy, a central bank would set target interest rates to have a negative value. This was first heard of in the 1990s and has only been used under extraordinary circumstances.

A negative interest rate implies that the central bank will charge you interest to deposit your cash with them. Rather than receiving deposits and paying the depositor interest, they charge the interest to the depositor, thus incentivizing a depositor to invest as much of their cash elsewhere as possible. For banks, negative interest incentivizes them to lend money more freely to avoid earning no interest on unused cash. In periods of deflation, businesses and people tend to hold their money, which causes a reduction in aggregate demand. If sustained, it can cause prices to fall further and halt real production. In such cases, the central bank needs an expansionary monetary policy to get the country out of economic stagnation.

Negative interest rates are a last resort effort to boost growth. Central banks turn to them when everything else fails. In theory, negative interest rates will lower borrowing costs for people and companies, drive demand for loans, and incentivize people to spend and invest. Retail banks can choose to internalize the costs of negative interest rates, but this affects their profits. They will weather this cost in cases where they don't want small depositors to withdraw their cash.

An example of negative interest rates would be for a central bank to set a benchmark rate of -0.2%. Banks depositing with the central bank would pay 0.2% for the privilege, thus incentivizing them to use the cash elsewhere. The Swiss Government ran such a regime at the beginning of the 1970s to counter the appreciation of their currency from investors running away from inflation in other parts of the globe. In 2010 and 2012, Sweden and Denmark used negative interest rates to deal with hot money flows into their countries. There were fears that banks and customers would remove all their money holdings, but that did not happen in either of those cases. Evidence suggests that they were all successful.

Of course, some risks and consequences are tied to negative interest rates. If banks penalize people for keeping savings, that might not affect retail customers or push them to spend more money. They may keep their money at home. Besides, these interest rates can inspire bank runs as people rush to avoid paying interest rates on their savings. Banks that want to prevent cash runs can avoid applying the interest rates on small deposits and apply them on large pension fund deposits, such as corporate clients. This would encourage corporate savers to invest in things that offer better returns while protecting the economy and banks from the effects of a bank run.

THE BASICS OF UNCONVENTIONAL MONETARY POLICIES

A monetary policy becomes unconventional when tools different from changing the policy interest rate are applied. These tools could be asset purchases, negative interest rates (as discussed earlier), forward guidance, term funding facilities, and adjusting operations in the market. All of these tools, except negative interest rates, have been in central banks' arsenals and used in some ways by central banks in the past, primarily to support financial markets. Their use as a principal mechanism for meeting monetary policy goals makes them a hot subject today.

In forward guidance, the central banks communicate a stance on monetary policy. They let the participants in the market, as well as the general public, know what the future of interest rates looks like. They may also choose to reveal other aspects of monetary policy. The central bank reserves the right to make monetary policy based on time or the state of the economy. If it is time-based, the bank will commit to keeping the interest rates at a certain level for a specified period. If it is based on the economy, the bank commits to a specific stance until certain economic conditions are achieved. During the COVID-19 pandemic, central banks instituted low policy interest rates to support the financial system and the economy. They also actively offered forward guidance to reinforce their commitment to financial stability. Generally, forward guidance helps to reduce uncertainty.

When the central bank intervenes through asset purchases, it often intervenes in the private sector to create central bank reserves. Some people refer to this as 'money printing,' but the central bank does not actually mint new money. Since the 2008 global financial crisis, asset purchases have been used more and have expanded the central banks' balance sheets. Furthermore, central banks have diversified the kinds of assets they buy, even though the primary type is still government bonds.

When a central bank decides to make asset purchases, it either sets a target for the amount of assets it will buy, regardless of price, or it sets a price target to buy whatever assets it can at that price. When the target is set as the quantity, it is called quantitative easing. The specific goal of asset purchases will vary based on the country. However, the common theme is that they are all about lowering the interest rates on risk-free assets across different maturities. Buying assets will decrease interest rates across the yield curve, not just the overnight rate. These purchases reinforce the forward guidance offered by the bank, adding downward pressure on yields. Investors will use the proceeds from asset sales to the central bank to buy other assets, causing a broad appreciation in asset prices.

Sometimes, central banks intervene through term funding facilities that offer financial institutions long-term funding at low costs. Generally, these facilities will be at costs below these institutions' existing sources. They are particularly beneficial when short-term interest rates are high as they lower the overall cost of funding. These facilities were used following the financial crisis of 2008. They make borrowing cheaper, more accessible and support the supply of credit. Term funding facilities also incentivize financial institutions to lend to people and businesses.

The final way a central bank may intervene could be through adjusting market operations. In response to a crisis, central banks change market operations to handle strains in the financial market. The interventions vary from country to country. However, they often amount to the central bank providing more liquidity, expanding collateral accepted from financial institutions, and allowing more counterparties to participate in domestic market operations. These changes usually aim to address financial institutions getting nervous about liquidity during a crisis, making them skittish about lending and investing. Adjusting market operations allows the central bank to create greater confidence among financial institutions for access to liquidity, which keeps financial markets running smoothly.

As a general rule, central banks put monetary policy in place to change the growth rate of the money supply and its size. They do this through interest rate adjustments, engaging in open market operations, and setting requirements for bank reserves. In an economic downturn, when these tools become limited and commercial banks start to worry about liquidity, central banks begin to employ other interventions that are unconventional. They enter the open market and purchase assets like MBSs in quantitative easing, and when that's not enough, they resort to negative interest rates. Of course, these actions have benefits, but they also come with risks.

THE RISKS AND BENEFITS OF UNCONVENTIONAL POLICIES

Evidence shows that most unconventional monetary policies have worked to date. It is worth noting that evaluating their impact is challenging, and one should always be careful with the conclusions they draw. When considering liquidity facilities applied by central banks, one can see how they have reduced yields and boosted activity in the targeted market. Often, these initiatives have the most considerable impact when accompanied by low access costs and flexible collateral requirements. For example, in 2009, the Federal Reserve ran an auction that caused a reduction in interbank market spreads and mitigated some of the difficulties in the funding market.

Besides, central bank dollar swaps tend to reduce stresses and minimize liquidity disruptions in the system. It seems that credit facilities have positively contributed to how targeted markets function and have helped to raise confidence. They signal that the central bank is willing to step in when needed. More specifically, measures targeting the short-term paper market in the UK, Japan, and the US have successfully increased issuance and lowered spreads. There is evidence to support the fact that introducing credit facilities positively impacts lending in financial markets. In the UK, because of these credit facilities, funding costs for banks have decreased, and conditions for credit have become more manageable. They have also triggered a reduction in interest rate premiums. It is possible that they mitigated a credit crunch post-2008. As if that was not enough, they improved market sentiment and allowed previously closed funding markets to reopen.

On a large scale, asset purchases do the financial markets a lot of good. The consensus among academia is that these purchases provide much-needed economic stimulus. In the United States, for example, the yields on mortgage bonds have reduced in response to asset purchases that the Federal Reserve made. They are now at record lows. In the same way, the estimated cumulative impact of the purchases in the US of 10-year bonds ranges up to 120 basis points. This is an impressive improvement. In Great Britain, the central bank purchases are estimated to have lowered yields by up to 100 basis points. In Japan, the story is similar—their quantitative easing program created a drop of 11 basis points. As a whole, asset purchases have been found to reduce the spreads of

European government bonds. However, that impact was only short-term. In the long run, the financial market stress re-emerged. Overall, it seems as if asset purchases are as effective as the underlying economic conditions under which they are performed.

There is research to suggest that besides asset purchases positively affecting financial markets, they also provide support to the economy to recover. They have contributed to price stability in the US by helping to stave deflation and disinflation. The evidence is the same when you look at the interventions of the Bank of England—there was a peak effect of up to a 2% increase in real output. Asset purchases have been effective, especially when the total purchased stock was significant compared to the target market and when the objectives and terms of those purchases were communicated clearly and transparently.

The effects appear mostly positive when central banks have used forward guidance. For example, since the Federal Reserve extended its commitment to keep the federal funds rate down, participants in the market have pushed back the date when they expect rates to start rising. If nothing else, this response proves that the financial market intervention is working. In Canada, a similar commitment helped change market players' expectations. After the bank's announcement, yields declined, and there was a strengthening in the growth and inflation in the country. However, while these policies seem to have many benefits, it is unclear how banks will exit from them, which is a major risk.

THE RISKS OF UNCONVENTIONAL POLICIES

One of the significant risks of unconventional monetary policies is how to manage the balance sheet and how to unwind. If a central bank unwinds too soon, that can undermine the economic recovery. It could create excess liquidity and contribute to inflation if it takes too long to unwind. It is a very tricky balance to figure out. Besides, banks must be committed to communicating clearly and providing guidance for any unwind to succeed. Even though the monetary base has expanded compared to many economies, inflation has been chiefly aligned with the objectives for price stability set by major central banks. Even expectations for inflation are anchored. However, an increase in liquidity should be managed well to avoid inflation in the future. How much monetary policy accommodation an economy can take can be lowered by increasing interest paid on reserves or reducing asset holdings on the balance sheet for the central bank. This means central banks must make asset sales or allow assets to mature instead of rolling them over.

At the same time, increasing policy rates and reducing reserves could change the system. The central bank must be careful about the whole process because an expanded balance sheet exposes the bank to potential loss. For example, today, the Federal Reserve could have to deal with losses in scenarios of asset sales. Additionally, buying riskier assets could create a capital loss, especially when coupled with relaxed collateral requirements for bank loans. Of course, in principle, central banks can bear these risks without impairing their ability to operate well. Losses would not prevent the central bank from tightening when the economy begins to recover, but they are still a risk worth considering.

Another risk of unconventional monetary policies appertains to the credibility and independence of the central bank. When the central bank buys government debt in rounds of asset purchases, it could undermine its credibility, especially when such purchases facilitate the government's enormous debts. This could make the bank lose its perceived independence and alter inflation expectations. Besides, the central bank's reputation could be damaged if it has significant losses in its portfolio. Central banks must ensure that their interventions are communicated well and only aimed at achieving necessary objectives. Otherwise, they are an unnecessary risk.

In many countries, banks have implemented balance sheet policies that extend the period of near-zero interest rates for the whole term structure. This is a cause for concern. Imagine an insurance company or a pension fund that is required or prefers to keep long-term assets in its portfolios. How will it be affected? Because of its need to match returns for these assets with its liabilities, the pension fund or insurance company may need to invest in riskier assets to earn a higher yield and match its liabilities. Portfolio rebalancing is a significant channel through which asset purchases work, but it could create excess risk and increase vulnerabilities within the financial system. Then, there will be a need for even heightened diligence among monetary policymakers.

Moreover, keeping interest rates low for an extended period could create forbearance because longer-dated loans allow nonviable banks or firms to keep operating. And how much better will the financial system be if it is littered with zombie financial institutions? How good will that be for the economy?

Another risk of unconventional monetary policies is the potential to create distributional effects from asset purchases. These purchases could end up helping one group at another group's expense. Low long-term yields tend to favor borrowers more than savers. Still, some economists argue that the effects tied to portfolio rebalancing could benefit people with equities more than those holding bonds. This concern may be overstated in cases where low yields get offset by the high prices of the assets, but it is still a risk to be mindful of.

Finally, there is the risk of spillovers. Like conventional policies, unconventional monetary policies can affect other prices in different asset markets. Asset purchases could reduce yields on bonds and the value of a country's currency. Central banks appear to be trying to depreciate their currency in emerging market economies and even in some industrialized economies.

The recession that followed the financial crisis of 2008 prompted a lot of central banks to put in place a series of unconventional policies that had never been tried before. Data has shown that these measures effectively mitigate the worst aspects of the financial crisis and boost recovery. Without them, the world's economy would be worse. Thus, these policies have become part of how central banks operate, allowing them to offer considerable policy stimulus when the situation demands it. Nevertheless, their risks need to be managed if their effectiveness is to be sustained. Central banks must consider how they will exit from these policies and bear their potential costs.

THE CONTROVERSIES SURROUNDING CENTRAL BANK INTERVENTIONS

All central banks, from the European Central Bank and the Federal Reserve to the Bank of England, from Oceania to Latin America and Africa, must figure out how to deal with the controversies surrounding their interventions. One of the main controversies has to do with their independence. Central banks like to wear their independence as a badge of honor, but people are no longer convinced that it means what it used to. The idea of an independent central bank started in the 20th century when independence meant that these central banks were free from the influence and direction of politicians. They would not bend to the interests and concerns of these politicians. Instead, central bankers were free to set monetary policy the way they believed to be best to bring inflation down and create financial stability. Economists call this anchoring price expectations.

The idea of independence came from judges who had to do the hard work of dispensing justice without independence, so they were given the freedom from the legislative and executive branches to do their job. When the value of money was divorced from the gold standard after the system's collapse in the 1970s, independent central banks guarded price stability. The idea was that many trade-offs needed to be made between unemployment and inflation. Without guidance, politicians and voters would choose low unemployment and higher inflation. However, the experience of the Great Depression showed that to be a short-sighted choice. Inflation can never remain steady. It would keep accelerating so much that what seemed like a good trade-off would soon become a dangerous instability and create economic chaos. Then, markets would respond by dumping assets. The foreign value of currencies would then spiral downwards.

Under the shadow of this scenario, the notion of the central bank's independence came up. The bank was supposed to act as an institution countering the majority.

It was mandated to do whatever it took to meet just one objective: keep inflation low. Giving the central bank this position was meant to deter reckless politicians from trying to implement expansive policies. The understanding was that politicians would know early enough that the central bank would be bound by duty to implement extreme interest rates. This would deter politicians but also send a message of reassurance to financial markets. It was understood that creating credibility would be painful, but it would be worth it when interest rates were lowered. That way, central banks could achieve price stability with a less harmful level of unemployment. You could not avoid this trade-off, but you could better the results by reassuring investors that their interests would be prioritized.

This was a model dependent on many assumptions about the economy. Firstly, that there was a connection between unemployment and inflation. Secondly, it was assumed that global financial markets could punish people. Thirdly, there was the underlying belief that overspending in politics was a better way to get votes. Finally, there was the assumption that society had many forces pushing for high levels of unemployment despite inflation. This model was also based on an unclear vision of modern history and at odds with politics because it made cynical assumptions about the motivations of politicians and voters. Even so, this was the system, and it worked for a while.

Now, the controversy is centered on the foundations of the central bank's independence. In recent days, central banks have become more influential and powerful. However, the expansion of their balance sheets and their role has not created more clarity or purpose. The increased responsibility and power has made the central bank appear less independent. Formal mandates have not been adjusted much, even though a vast expansion is possible. In the US, for example, where the extension has been very dramatic, it can only be quantified as a transformation of the state, which has happened only when needed and under the pressure of a crisis, with little opportunity for debate.

This begs the question—are central banks genuinely independent? There used to be a time when that independence was sacrosanct. It guaranteed an authority and perspective filled with accountability and responsibility around a well-articulated and nonpolitical goal. The questioning of liberal democracies and authoritarianism have applied pressure on central bankers, polarizing appointments and touting removal from office as a possibility. Of course, some of the politicization may be justified because there is little clarity in the central bank mandates. The philosophy of economics and markets seems to have moved from central banks.

It does not help that some individual central bankers appear to want political roles and the influence that comes with them. Fundamentally, these forces change what should be considered good governance and shift power internally to boards instead of individuals. It creates a governance system through bodies like financial stability committees and gives more power to institutions like courts. The consequence is that the typical central bank loses power, ironically, at a time when it is considered the most potent economic factor in every country.

Another controversy surrounding central bank interventions is the clarity of their mandate. Many central banks are structurally losing their independence and the clarity of their assignment. They are expected to meet social and partly political duties without the necessary power or legitimacy. The central bank's job used to be clear—to keep prices stable and hit an inflation target. With time, this mandate started changing. It grew toward dual mandates such as job creation and economic growth, and these mandates lost the preciseness of their targets.

One wonders whether the central bank's mandate is still stable or if it is about managing a dynamic economy. How does stability work in a world where disruption is a positive trait and is the graveyard for stability? Perhaps, central banks should now exist to smooth the cycle and try to reconcile stability and dynamism. Whatever the case, it is clear that its mandate has never been more clouded, especially in periods of crisis when its actions often appear to favor shareholders and elites, creating inequality. Part of this controversy is the suspicion that the central bank mandates cannot remain purely technical because their impacts touch all areas of life, from environmental action and social well-being to sustainability and industrial policies. People on the proponent side of this debate are unhappy that central banks are creating losers and winners in the economic world and making their mandate more ambiguous and complex.

A third controversy hinges on the question of neutrality. Are the responsibilities of the central bank truly politically or socially neutral? It is hard to imagine that they are. Keeping interest rates low for a long time has made life comfortable for some banks. However, it has also affected how sustainable pension funds are, affecting many people and favoring private actors looking for yield. Not only that, but one cannot see the emergency actions of the central bank as neutral—like the sudden social responsibility to be a lender of last resort. Social trust in central banks is affected, and so are the expectations people have of the banks to act responsibly to maintain the financial health of an economy, protect the consumer, be climate conscious, and deal with social inequalities.

Today, we expect central banks to be socially responsible, and this has come at a time when the banks appear to be losing some of their clout. Of course, this means people wonder whether the banks are using their substantial balance sheets strategically. Their low interest rates are helping some people and hurting others, so is that socially neutral? Arguably, this is one of the most complex controversies because debaters agree on some issues, like the vital role the central banks play in the economy and future of the country.

I hope you're enjoying *A Brief History of Central Banking*. If you have any feedback, whether positive or negative, please consider leaving a review. My goal is to provide the best possible books for you, and your reviews are crucial in achieving that.

5

THE FUTURE OF CENTRAL BANKING:

CHALLENGES AND OPPORTUNITIES

> "*The best way to predict the future is to create it.*"
>
> — **PETER DRUCKER**

Once again, central banks find themselves challenged to reinvent themselves in response to global events. There have been new waves of disruption since the global financial crisis, and each imposes new reflections on how central banks need to be operating in the world and their interactions with stakeholders. Just think about Europe for a second. There are many fast and fundamental changes driven by the EU agenda, from green and sustainable developments based on the Green Deal to the goal of showcasing digital leadership all over the globe. These trends have implications for central banks across Europe, some stretching the banks beyond their traditional roles and forcing them to look at their models for maintaining financial and monetary stability to see if they work. They must consider their contributions to a society trying to address some of its biggest challenges.

For example, central banks must embrace or, at the very least, explore new and innovative ways to engage with market participants. They will need to reframe how they supervise new players, like those in tech, with their disruptive models for doing business. New players are not like traditional businesses in how they operate. They do not typically have large loans or deposits on their balance sheets. They tend to work as market intermediaries, offering new technologies, and they seem to be growing in their role within the financial system. Because of this, central banks will have to adjust how they provide supervision. They must understand new business models and how the new participants use technological tools. Central banks would be wise to consider taking part in discussions with FinTech to iron out the issues early enough in the life cycles of these businesses so that they can offer guidance toward sustainable and compliant growth.

Secondly, the future central bank cannot afford to ignore nonperforming loans. According to data from the European Commission, nonperforming loans are expected to increase in the years to come. At the same time, businesses and individuals cannot afford to lose their access to funding. The ECB estimates these loans could reach as high as €1.4 trillion in Europe. Other parts of the world register similar alarming numbers. Central banks of the future will have to figure out what actions to take to grow their secondary debt markets, solve corporate insolvency, and deal with the legislation for debt recovery. They will have to find ways to support asset management companies and implement measures to help the public ensure funding remains uninterrupted. All these goals are lofty, but central banks must pull up their socks. They will also need to find ways to use technology to analyze their portfolios and predict the possibility of nonperforming loans in specific sectors. To catch patterns early enough, they must embrace technology transformation, completely overhauling their IT systems to improve efficiency and delivery in the digital economy. Ideally, with better tech, they could analyze and interpret data in real-time and pick out any deviations before they morph into a financial crisis.

Thirdly, and perhaps obviously, future central banks will have to embrace or, at the very least, consider digital currencies. All over the world, central banks are looking into CBDCs (Central Bank Digital Currencies), with some of them having already issued digital currencies. In Europe, the ECB has prioritized the digital euro. The bank already declared that the digital euro would be an e-version of the existing euro, not to replace it, but to go with it, giving more choices for making payments to consumers. Adopting digital currencies will challenge the banks, pushing how they operate, their process designs, and their monetary policy to change. For example, central banks will be forced to find ways to mitigate cyber risk. They will have to keep their currencies compliant with the rules for data protection. They will also need to consider how these digital currencies affect interest rates, asset prices, and exchange rates and find ways to index these currencies to one price index rather than having constant sustained value like coins or cash. They will have to seriously consider how these currencies affect the financial sector.

It is not inconceivable that a visible and intentional engagement with issues of climate change will mark the central bank of the future. This has already started to happen. Central banks do not directly make climate policy but can participate significantly through their monetary policy. They tend to have a responsibility to do it, as well as opportunities, which will be discussed more toward the end of this chapter, to drive change in the climate issue. Recently, the ECB launched a new climate change center and started acting to understand the way the expansion of the financial system affects the climate. In the US, supervisors of the Federal Reserve expressed an expectation that banks would implement strategies to help them find, measure, control, and maintain their material risks, which also extend to climate risks.

The central bank of the future strives toward going green. This is one of the goals of the Green Deal in the EU. These banks are committed to accelerating accountable finance, and controlling environmental risk will be central to how they do that. Remember that climate change directly affects the stability of a financial system, so that's a big incentive for central banks to care. They will have climate integrated into their economic risk assessments and find ways to incentivize green finance. These central banks will buy assets that are geared toward going green. They will create models that can measure environmental risks involved in development, among many other climate-conscious actions.

Finally, the central bank of the future will be greatly concerned with inclusion and diversity. These two principles have become very big in our society today, and central banks, being cornerstones in our community, face the same issues surrounding them that other organizations do. Like other organizations, central banks need to attract the best talent, but future central banks will have to figure out how to do this while fostering inclusion and diversity. They may have to consider geographical representation as part of diversity, for example, something important to institutions in the EU. They will need to consider things like gender parity. To find the correct answers to the challenges they are facing, central banks will need to be able to rely on a diverse talent pool, looking at things like capabilities, age, and gender.

As central banks evolve toward the future, as I have just described, their organizational structure, roles, and strategies will change from what they have been in the past. To start with, central banks will have to implement new regulatory and supervisory technological tools to support how they supervise market participants. They will need to rethink their partnerships with other institutions. In the future, central banks will steadily walk toward digital currencies and embrace state-of-the-art tech to analyze financial data in real-time. They will be a preferred employer for the best talent in the market and grow in how they communicate their role and expectations of the market players.

To deal with the challenges of the future all over the world, central banks will have to work closely with other policymakers and authorities. They may remain regulators but more oriented toward innovation, requiring technological transformation and a cultural shift to welcome better relationships with the whole ecosystem. In the future, the central bank will play an evolving role in maintaining financial and monetary stability while helping to create a technological, inclusive, and sustainable world. To achieve this, the central bank must grapple with a significant issue today—populism.

THE EMERGENCE AND RISE OF POPULISM

New political movements are changing the way political systems in industrialized democracies operate. For starters, the way political conflict unfolds has adjusted. Traditionally, redistributive and economic conflict was between the left and the right, but that division is waning. It is replaced by a new division between conservative, socially conservative, and nationalist groups versus socially progressive and cosmopolitan ones. You can spot these changes by looking at voting outcomes, for example, and how political parties are positioned. Secondly, traditional social democratic parties do not enjoy as much support as they used to. New parties have appeared with a rather peculiar take on political conflict. Many of these parties, commonly called populists, take anti-elite and anti-establishment platforms, claiming to speak to the people's true interests.

None of these changes are independent. Traditional parties struggle to position themselves in the new world of political conflict because they fear losing their support base or because there are genuine blocks to such changes. Others worry that their policy promises would not be credible in these new dimensions. As a result, there is a political vacuum that is getting filled by unknown parties. To stamp their stances and draw to the less educated, these new parties have embraced populist rhetoric. It helps their cause that, most times, these new politicians are indeed outsiders in the labor markets, social environments, and political system.

But why is this happening now? Some theories have been put forward to explain this phenomenon. The cultural backlash theory says that the more traditional and less educated voters are finally reacting to seeing their value system eroded in a society they find too cosmopolitan and aggressive. Others suggest that the populist parties are a reaction to economic trouble. Some data looking at voting outcomes found that populist support was correlated with financial distress, a loss of social standing, and severe trade shocks.

Both explanations may capture some aspects of the problem. Even so, there is a puzzle that needs solving. In the past, economic trouble had people demanding to be protected through state welfare, and this helped democratic parties and made trade unions stronger. Why is the opposite happening now? Why are economic shocks pushing voters toward more conservative voters who campaign on retrenching state welfare, for example? Even though there is significant economic inequality and decreasing social mobility, those most affected care more about civil rights and immigration than they are concerned about redistribution. Sometimes they support policies that are opposed to their economic interests.

A likely answer to these puzzles is that this points to a shift of parties in favor of deregulation and progressive policies that neglect the interests and wishes of traditional supporters. Without political options, people not benefiting from tech advances and globalization resort to populism. Its rise is a global phenomenon that cannot be explained as a consequence of policy mistakes made by mainstream politicians alone. There has to be more to the story. It is possible that this shift has to do with the demand side of politics. The nature of politics is opposition—us versus them. But who are 'they,' and who are 'we?' In the past, these distinctions were based on class and the left and right divide. Economic and social changes have raised the relevance of a difference based on education and cultural attitudes. Tech and globalization have made the distinction more relevant because the cultural and educational divide separates winners and losers.

According to social psychologists, these categorizations have caused a restructuring in the social world and created cognitive distortions. By nature, we make our differences too simple and exaggerated. But, as we identify with a specific group, we change our beliefs to fit in. So, if the 'us' is the working class, then the 'them' is the bourgeoisie. A left-wing person will exaggerate the gains of redistributive taxation, while the opponent will take the opposite conviction. As social groups that are politically relevant change, so do policy attitudes and belief distortions so that if 'them' is the highly educated elite in urban areas, then 'us' is the less educated provincial resident. Our conflict is about immigration, civil rights, and globalization. We have become more polarized on these issues.

Switching our social identities and the changes that flow from that can explain the connection between economic distress and the waning support for economic redistribution. The shocks that have hit the less educated and socially conservative have made them seem more similar. They have made them feel like the losers of technology and globalization. Their exaggerated perception of group conflict has shaped their policy demands.

These changes have happened over a long period. The rise of populism has accelerated in the last decade, coinciding with two main events—the global financial crisis and social media diffusion. The two events have likely contributed to the proliferation of populism. The role social media has played still needs to be studied. Still, it is likely that the disintermediation of traditional information sources has amplified emotional reactions and strengthened stereotyping. It has facilitated direct contact between political leaders and citizens, reducing entry barriers for new political organizations.

As for the financial crisis, it cannot be a coincidence that populism accelerated immediately after the recession. A sort of radicalized political conflict always followed economic crises in the past and gave rise to extremist parties. This is not new. A financial crisis is easy to blame on the economic and political establishment. The result is a loss of trust in the mainstream parties and existing institutions and a movement toward new political leaders.

Moreover, populist politicians tend to be risky because they are untested and support unconventional policies. This riskiness makes them attractive to people already disappointed by the system. The risk promises to give them a chance to recover what they lost.

HOW POPULISM AFFECTS CENTRAL BANKS

It appears as though populism is not a transitory idea. Technological advances and globalization are here to stay, and so is populism. The cultural and educational divide associated with them will change but not be reversed. At the same time, increased polarization and the fall of social mobility may reinforce anti-establishment ideas. Expectedly, these changes will have a profound effect on political systems. Nearly everywhere, party systems organized in terms of the right and left divide will begin to change.

New parties will join in proportional electoral systems, and this change will strengthen more populist parties. The outcomes will be harder to predict in majoritarian systems like the UK and the US. Either way, the political system will get a new dimension. This second dimension overlaps with either being for or against political and economic establishments. After the dust has settled, who is to know whether the changes will be for good?

Someone may argue that populism will improve the conditions for the losers of globalization and make economic outcomes more inclusive and equitable. Populism may create inconsistent and counterproductive policies creating a risk of policy mistakes.

The policy mistakes risk will be enhanced by things like the bias against redistribution often connected with populism, an urgency to get immediate results which creates short-sighted policies, and political extremism characterized by radical policies which encourage more risk-taking. Moreover, the spread of nationalism creates another threat to world order. Some of the most challenging policy issues demand global solutions. Nationalist populists will advocate for the dismantling of national organizations. Instead of moving us forward, that will take us backward. This is the most significant danger of populism—it will take world order in a direction opposite to where we want to be.

But what exactly is populism, and how will these effects trickle down to central banks? The standard definition characterizes populism as the deep suspicion of some groups of people against a prevailing establishment. According to populist sentiment, the establishment in view does not rule for the common good but is conspiring against people. It goes on to place these people as the repositories for the soul of the nation, not establishments. A populist opposes checks and balances and any institutional constraints on political power from autonomous institutions.

A good example would be the independence of the central bank. By nature, an independent central bank takes decision power away from politicians, so they cannot do much to influence monetary policy or interventions. A populist sees this as socially detrimental. They would regard the central bank's independence and mandate to pursue price stability as something to rally against because they do not like monetary dominance.

Because they would be attacking institutions (like the central bank) that they consider constraining, one cost of populism can be damaging these institutions and the market economy. This can be true of the rule of law, state institutions, the stability of central banks, institutions that safeguard international collaboration like the IMF and the World Bank, an open economic exchange like WTO, or fiscal rules meant to ensure sustainability. As it is, the central bank has gone through many changes because of financial and sovereign debt issues. In many countries, central banks were the primary safeguard for financial stability. They used powerful tools to help economic recovery and ease fiscal debt. Most were mandated with extra roles in macro and micro-prudential surveillance. All of these roles will be affected by the rise of populism.

Populist governments share features like a distrust for mainstream institutions and economics, thinking only of the short term, a distrust toward globalization, nationalism, and a neglect of facts and analysis. These aversions create tension with the mandate and operation of independent central banks, which tend to be mainstream, globalist, liberal, and science and fact-based. It remains to be seen whether any attempts to interfere with the operation of central banks will be reflected in more comprehensive changes to central bank laws. It is the damage inflicted on institutions like the central bank, which are at the heart of open market economies and financial order, which could have the most severe impact on global economic development.

THE CHALLENGES OF MAINTAINING FINANCIAL STABILITY IN A GLOBALIZED ECONOMY

The last five decades have seen the financial system experience unprecedented changes. These changes started with the regime change of the 1970s for most major currencies into flexible exchange rates. That shift alone made foreign exchange markets, for example, more efficient and more accurate as a gauge of the expectations of the market players of the future. Then derivatives and secondary markets for governments and other fixed-income securities started deepening and broadening. Thanks to technology, market information could flow in a timelier manner. Private transactors in industrialized countries began learning to deal with different risk types.

New financial product markets expanded to enable agents to lay off risks or give them an edge.

As these things happened, central banks realized that the informational and legal framework necessary for efficient financial markets must be extended and refined. Financial markets and institutions also needed a level of deregulation and liberalization. In the early 1970s, algorithms (specifically for option pricing) were developed to handle complex financial products. Because of these innovations, markets in developed countries have drawn closer and closer to the ideals—effectively managing risk and allocating resources across regions and sectors over time to ensure financial stability.

Still, the work of keeping a globalized economy financially stable is difficult. For example, a benefit of a globalized economy is that transaction fees associated with doing business are lower, thus encouraging financial institutions to offer more services and lend more freely. It is, therefore, more straightforward for them to distribute risk more effectively. The short-term result of this is efficiency gains that increase financial activity by businesses, governments, and individuals and create a global financial system that looks more robust and resistant to economic shocks coming from other countries. Yet, this does not seem to be the case when considering the state of financial markets today. After the 2008 recession, if that trend were accurate in the long term, global output growth would have remained stable, and global inflation would have been lower. One wonders where the disconnect between theoretical facts and reality comes from.

Secondly, while the globalized and liberalized financial system is more elastic than it was, it is still not immune from creating economic imbalances, which have produced many close calls. Just think about the many systemic banking crises that affected emerging market, and some industrialized, countries since the dot-com bubble of the 90s and the debt crises of Argentina and Russia. It would seem that the tremendous strides central banks have made in developing the global financial system are still unable to overcome the inherent tendency for lenders and borrowers to alternate between periods of unjustified pessimism and excess exuberance about the future. To ensure financial stability, the central bank has to deal with this truth, anticipate it, and manage it efficiently so that it does not topple all efforts to move forward.

These challenges are compounded by the supervisory challenges within the central banking system, which must be sorted out to enhance financial stability. Many of these challenges come from a slow and steady buildup of economic imbalances over time, especially when macro-economic performance seems solid. Financial inequality is a significant and persistent deviation from known financial variables for an extended period. Admittedly, this is not the most scientific definition. Still, it captures the truth that dynamic market processes can accumulate over time as you build on market expectations, even though the considered variables are mean-reverting. These imbalances can return to the market and manifest as real sector behavior.

Based on neo-Keynesian theory, which deals with stability and economic growth instead of full employment, analyzing these imbalances does not play a major role. Future expectations were central to these theories of the efficiency of capital and liquidity preferences. Still, the theory's prescriptions focused only on optimizing fiscal and monetary policies. However, globalization has made it so that economic analysis is now relevant. Here, I am referring to the practice which emphasizes the function of expectations in driving the evolution of a capitalist market economy and focuses on the changing processes through which financial imbalances can accumulate over time. Specifically, this approach emphasizes misallocations of resources tied to excessive credit expansion and a buildup of debt over time, which could ultimately become impossible to bail out.

Interestingly, the literature on this issue before the Second World War raised the possibility that optimizing policy in the short run could create long-term problems by creating more considerable financial imbalances, partly through moral hazard. The crucial role of any policy is to govern its field so that, given time, there will be no market excesses. It should give market participants a transparent view of its objectives and the general direction the policymakers expect the economy to go. Central banks are still figuring out how to create and communicate such a policy.

It is easy to see that the world is dealing with unprecedented external and internal imbalances. If we were to make a list of these imbalances, we would have to start with the level of policy interest rates. Until recently, real policy rates were nearly zero in the US. They remain below the recommended long-term neutral rate. In continental Europe and Asia, these rates are still near zero. In Japan, the nominal interest rate has stayed at zero for a long time, and QE has increased the bank's balance sheet to more than 30% of GDP. Typically, the interest rates set by financial markets for the long term are low, which creates a problem.

Moreover, these challenges have led to unusually low corporate and sovereign credit spreads and market volatility measures. There have also been some imbalances connected to the reductions in household savings rates in many industrialized countries. Typically, this trend is accompanied by increases in individual debt levels. In major developed economies, the current levels of fiscal deficits create a question of sustainability. This is happening in an environment where many industrial countries are recording an increase in housing prices to record levels.

On a global scale, one has to begin in the US when considering the imbalances. In the US, an account deficit has been rising as a percentage of GDP for decades. The net service account is negative, reflecting that the wealthiest country in the world also has the biggest international debt burden. Simply put, we do not have to look far to see financial imbalances in the global financial system. One must consider some of their possible causes to understand their implications. Some of these domestic imbalances come from three major structural shifts that have affected both emerging and industrial countries, and those internal imbalances have caused external imbalances.

SHIFTS IN THE FINANCIAL SYSTEM AND THEIR ASSOCIATED COMPLICATIONS

The first one of these shifts is the liberalization of institutions and markets in the financial system discussed earlier. Today, there are many market sources for credit in industrial countries. People can get money from financial intermediaries, and it is possible to achieve risk transfer in many ways. Without a doubt, this has many benefits. For example, intense competition among institutions and markets has given people more choices and reduced the cost of loans, making life easier for savers and providing more accessible credit to borrowers.

However, evidence suggests another unfavorable byproduct. The internal risk measures in banks, asset prices, loan loss provisions, credit spreads, and the ratings generated by the new unofficial agencies all move up or down based on economic activity. This tendency of the financial system to fluctuate affects the economy in a way that can increase instabilities in economic activity, costs, prices, and aggregate demand. Credit can increase asset prices on consumer durables or fixed investments. These developments will eventually trace back to raised expectations of future profits. This creates the danger of a self-reinforcing system of irrational exuberance.

The second shift that has created imbalances is connected with the real sector of the economy. When markets are liberalized for services, goods, and factors of production globally, more so in economies that had been centrally planned, that creates a positive supply shock with a disinflationary effect on the global economy and affects some economies within the market. Just think about it; in recent years, the prices of services and goods and the changes in work practices and wages have increased contestability all over the globe.

Thirdly, the last few decades have seen an increased focus (for monetary authorities and their practices, particularly in industrial economies) on keeping price stability in the form of stable, predictable, and low inflation. We know the perks of low inflation, but the other shifts have created incredible complications. While inflation is under control, it might look like there is no need for monetary tightening, even with rapid credit growth. However, this also means there is less control over the ups and downs in the financial system. A more flexible and open financial system has more potential for fluctuations; without enough measures to manage these, it could cause instability. One could argue that the 'search for yield' in periods with low interest rates speeds up this process.

If these forces explain the unusual imbalances central banks in developed economies have to deal with, they also have relevance for emerging markets. The easy monetary conditions in developed economies are reducing exchange rates for their developed markets. More so the dollar. But they also impose upward pressure on rates for emerging economies, especially in Asia. Emerging markets can try to resist these pressures. However, in a disinflationary environment, the many interventions of the central bank and the challenges in managing their downsides make it a bit difficult. It doesn't help that when foreign exchange reserves flow back to developed economies, it further adds to the financial fluctuations. To maintain financial stability in a post-Bretton Woods world, central banks must deal with a worldwide problem of excess liquidity.

It is a fact that the countries that have the largest current deficits—the UK, the US, New Zealand, and Australia—are also often the ones with the largest fiscal imbalances. They tend to have low savings rates and enduring housing booms. Because they also have high asset prices, they are perceived as being wealthy and being more significant spenders, but domestic absorption eventually exceeds production, and they increase their current deficit. Central banks must analyze this issue to determine why some countries are more prone to internal imbalances than others. They have to handle both the dangers and the benefits of financial liberalization, which begs the question—why is this a challenge?

If all the possible internal imbalances arise, they could create a crisis within the financial system. It may be hard to predict where and when the stretched system will fail. It is also possible that if there is less demand for assets denominated in US dollars overseas, for example, regardless of the reason, the dollar would depreciate, and interest rates in the world would increase. The prices for some real and financial assets would reduce, and these adjustments could create a deflationary environment. The world would enter a long period characterized by slow growth, reinforced by a reduction in the capital of market participants, including financial institutions that would reduce their supply of credit. That has happened in the past, and it can happen again. Central banks trying to keep financial stability in a globalized economy must remember this.

All these challenges are interconnected, so they make for a very complex global financial system. One wonders whether policy can help central banks walk the taut lines to maintain financial stability. That's a complicated question because even if imbalances can cause macro problems, the costs of these problems could be massive. The obvious recommendation to tighten interest rates to deal with financial excesses could stand in the way of economic growth.

Fortunately, some countries have no obvious constraints to tightening policy. In the US, for instance, the Federal Reserve has been increasing policy interest rates gradually as of mid-2023, and that has been constraining imbalances and reducing inflation. The other issue is implementing government policies that allow businesses, individuals, or entities to reduce the amounts they owe over time. This is no easy feat. How does the central bank figure out the proper measures to do this without depreciating their currency while keeping inflation at bearable levels?

In a world where we are all connected, central banks must consider internal and external factors to maintain financial stability. They have to operate as part of the global financial system, not just as stewards of a domestic economy. Keeping the financial system even is no longer a direct and simple affair that can be solved with interventions alone. Globalization has created a complex financial system dominated by a market that craves yield, more capacity, increased scope to act, and destabilizing sentiments of gloom and euphoria. Central banks have to deal with new combinations of factors and tail risks that could affect the real economy, and that is arguably the biggest challenge to achieving their mandate.

OPPORTUNITIES FOR INNOVATION AND COLLABORATION IN THE WORLD OF CENTRAL BANKING

It appears that the challenges presented by a globalized economy, in some ways, also provide opportunities for central banks to innovate and work with other market players to shape a future for everyone. Some of the apparent opportunities for collaboration and innovation include:

- Using AI

For a while now, banks have used artificial intelligence for credit scoring. Insurers have relied on AI to detect fraud and for underwriting. Central banks can figure out how to use AI to make things like credit analysis easier. They could also use AI to increase effectiveness through predictive analytics. At the very least, they could ensure financial institutions use AI responsibly and fairly.

- Taking advantage of machine learning

Machine learning has many potential applications in the data central banks have to process. For example, they can provide customized risk assessments in real-time. For instance, central banks can recognize early warning signs of nonperforming loans through machine learning. They can use this knowledge to inform their interventions during crises and help them preserve financial stability.

- Collaborating with FinTech

Technological innovation, led by FinTech companies, is changing the financial sector. Financial services have become digitized, making it more straightforward for financial institutions to increase their reach and grow their global footprint. It has opened doors for new players and enabled cross-border connectivity. Central banks can spearhead FinTech projects that pilot the integration of these advances. For example, they could lead the development of integrated platforms for reporting. That way, supervisors can assess risks by applying tech to unstructured data.

6

THE DARK SIDE OF CENTRAL BANKING:

CONSPIRACY THEORIES AND MISINFORMATION

> *"In a time of universal deceit, telling the truth is a revolutionary act."*
>
> — **GEORGE ORWELL**

Regardless of your worldview, some things are indisputable. One of those realities is that the last couple of years have seen unprecedented central bank and government interventions worldwide. Some governments have banked on the idea of safety to play a more prominent role in financial markets. At the same time, some central banks have used the consequences of their interventions to increase the supply of fiat currencies. Even when the world was preparing for the Second World War, central bank interventions did not reach the scale they are currently at. This has created complex ideological, moral, economic, psychological, and public health implications and made the debate around central banking far from simple.

In the face of such complexity, one must wonder which direction central banking will lead us. As it is, few institutions evoke more mythology and emotion than global central banks. The Federal Reserve, being the central bank of the world's largest economy, garners special attention. Central banks have power and influence, but some hyperbole in discussions surrounding them creates misunderstandings and births conspiracy theories. This chapter will deal with some of those myths, highlighting the hidden truths, and conclude by considering some of the possible reasons these myths and conspiracy theories come up in the first place.

MYTHS AND LEGENDS SURROUNDING CENTRAL BANKS

1. Central banks control the money supply, and CBDCs are tools for mass control.

This myth comes from many years of academic misunderstanding and poor economic theory. The proponents of this myth will say that central banks set the quantity of reserves. Then, banks multiply the reserves, producing them as loans so that the central bank directly controls how much money is created. However, past financial crises have taught us that this view is backward. Banks make loans first before they find reserves. Central banks accommodate the number of loans by offering the needed quantity reserves.

Consequently, the money multiplier that many people have become familiar with is a lie. Central banks do not have direct control over the deposits or quantity of loans. Private banks control loans and deposits.

It is worth mentioning that many central bank policies, like quantitative easing, are not really 'money printing' in the practical sense. They involve creating reserve deposits swapped for treasury bonds. When QE is reversed (quantitative tightening) and the bonds are sold to investors, or when the bonds mature, the money digitally created to undertake QE disappears, leaving the overall amount of money in the economy unchanged. You don't need more money for QE; you are just changing the composition of similar asset quantities.

Taken a step further, especially when you introduce CBDCs, this myth births another complex debate that CBDCs are the government's way of trying to control everything we do. This is an understandable theory; because of all the changes ahead, CBDCs appear to be the most likely candidate for the convergence of monetary policy and government. To understand this debate, we must look outside banking for a minute. Toward the end of the 16th century, English philosopher Jeremy Bentham developed controversial social reform ideas. He believed that power should be unverifiable and visible. Remember the time you were in school? How did you behave when the principal entered the class? Kids would work harder and straighten up because the principal was there. What if the principal was always there? They would not specifically be watching you throughout, but you would know they were there.

This is the power of behavioral psychology and what informed Bentham's panopticon. The panopticon was a concept for Bentham but became a central observation tower in prison cells. The guard was able to see every cell from the tower, but inmates could not see the tower. Prisoners never knew for sure whether or not they were watched. Bentham believed that all social groups could be changed through constant surveillance. The industry would be invigorated, health preserved, and morals reformed by simple observation.

The philosophers like Michel Foucault, who disagreed with Bentham's philosophy, believed that the panopticon would only ensure an automatic functioning of power. It was cruel to the prisoners. Foucault compared the panopticon to a town under an instruction to quarantine because of a plague. Officials must separate everyone and ensure villagers do not leave their homes and get exposed. Anyone caught outside is punished with death, ironic because the plague kills you anyway. In this village, constant surveillance regulates your daily life—even the minutest details.

Over time, there has been unease about this kind of monitoring. The first time concerns were raised was in the late 80s when personal computers came up, and people feared an information panopticon. Today, employers get programs tracking keystrokes to see how staff work. Parents get software that monitors phone usage for their kids. Governments are passing laws to collect data on suspected terrorists. Even public transport cards may monitor your physical movements. This kind of monitoring is analogous to the panopticon because it is one-way. As you work on your computer or scroll down your newsfeed, information is compiled and sent to someone else.

In that scenario, the computer is the panopticon tower, and you are the subject. Nothing is communicated to you. Your actions and online behavior can always be seen, but you will never get any information from the observer. The EU has tried to sort this problem with a regulation called 'the right to an explanation.' Users have the right to ask to know how algorithms make choices. That way, they can challenge the decisions or decide to opt-out. In this debate, one-way communication and lack of transparency always gain the most attention, with people arguing that they are about control.

Now imagine the same arguments for and against digital money, particularly CBDCs. Which side will you pick? Admittedly, things get scarier. What happens when a government can instantaneously see every aspect of your financial life? What if it can flip a switch and freeze every transaction and asset? Some people say it would be a necessary evil because it would help combat modern evils like terrorists and cartels, but what if the government got something wrong? It becomes the old balance between regulating behavior for a good society or giving the government a massive hammer at its discretion.

The answers to these questions are not obvious; otherwise, there would be no debate. One has to consider the implications of the developments we are making as a society, especially in an era where tools and technology seem to have outstripped our ability to consider domino effects carefully. We can begin by clarifying what we know about CBDCs so that, at the very least, the debate is not marred by misinformation. We know for sure that central banks adopt CBDCs for safety. The central bank can create a highly secured CBDC ecosystem so that we would not need other brokers. They would be efficient and with fewer risks. CBDCs would be able to compete in the world's financial markets, and they would be transparent, bringing a part of the economy out of the shadows. Consequently, users would feel more confident about the financial system.

As you can see, CBDCs bring good things for the central banks and their users. But one wonders, is it good not to need brokers or commercial banks? Operations with digital currencies may be cheaper, but do we want that? Would it help our everyday life? It doesn't help that

CBDCs are programmable, which means that they can expire. In China, for example, people have to use the digital yuan before a specific date, after which the Bank of China revokes it. Governments get to see how you use your money and can instantly take it from you under any circumstances. How good is this for personal freedom? Many questions still surround the question of digital currencies, and their possible downsides must be accounted for, but at least we can rest the myth that governments are trying to control everything we do through CBDCs.

2. Central banks 'manipulate' interest rates.

It is common to hear it said of central banks that they 'manipulate interest rates.' Like other myths, this one has a grain of truth and misinformation. It is based on the idea that interest rates would be better if they were left to the private market rather than controlled by a government entity. Unfortunately, people who push this myth do not know how central banking and banking generally work. A central bank is not just a central clearinghouse to settle payments. Before there were payments through central banks, bank-to-bank transactions relied on private clearinghouses. The problem with this was that banks stopped making payments whenever there was a financial panic, and that would make the depression worse. The clearinghouse could do nothing to help the situation.

In the case of a central bank, it leverages the powers of the government to make sure that panics do not create a situation that worsens a financial depression. A perfect example of this would be the financial crisis of 2008. When banks in the US stopped lending to one another, the Fed stepped in as a lender of last resort. Even if many banks at the time were not solvent, many people could still get their necessities through the banking system because most banks kept running, thanks to the help of the Fed. Imagine how events would have played out if the Fed had not lent money to those banks. The crisis would have bankrupted them, affecting even the largest banks and toppling the economy. The crisis would have been more catastrophic. You would not get anything unless you had money buried under a mattress.

To do its job as the central clearinghouse, the Fed must set an overnight rate for lending to other banks. Because most banks use the Fed system, they try to lend their deposits to other banks. This creates downward pressure on overnight interest rates because the system is closed, and banks cannot lend out their reserves in aggregate. As a result, the natural interest rate is 0% in the Fed funds market. This means that the central bank has to push rates higher than that. This is a mathematical reality in the closed system in which banks operate. Therefore, rates above 0% are always higher than the overnight rate—to say that the Fed never manipulates rates down. It constantly drives short-term rates up from 0%.

It is noteworthy that even though the overnight rate matters to overnight loans, many other factors influence different interest rates. The banking system determines most other rates based on creditworthiness. For example, your credit card and mortgage rates are a function of your creditworthiness. The overnight rate defines the base rate at which banks lend to each other; however, a spread is added on for all more risky loans. In addition, central banks determine the overnight rate by considering the economy's health and the banking system. They set it as a response to the economy. Banks set other rates based on product demand and creditworthiness.

Remembering that central banks set the overnight rate by gauging the economy's expected and current state is helpful. They have to estimate the direction the economy is going, which is not an easy job. In this sense, central banks are reactive. When inflation is low, interest rates also tend to be low. When it heats up, central banks generally raise rates in tandem to dampen the chances of inflation spiraling out of control. This may appear like control or manipulation, but it is more like a man keeping a dog on a leash. We could, of course, operate without this role of the central bank as a clearinghouse, but we have already found it to work. Flaws in the clearinghouse system aggravated the 1907 panic and the 1819, 1837, and 1873 depressions.

Essentially, the myth that central banks manipulate interest rates stems from a misunderstanding of the role and function of central banks in the economy. While it is true that central banks have the authority to set certain interest rates, it is essential to note that they do not do so arbitrarily or for their benefit. They are responsible for implementing monetary policy, which involves managing the money supply and influencing interest rates to achieve specific economic objectives, such as price stability, economic growth, and employment. One of the major tools they use to accomplish these objectives is manipulating short-term interest rates.

Typically, central banks set a target interest rate, like the US federal funds rate or the repo rate in India (the rate commercial banks get when borrowing money from the central bank). By adjusting this rate, central banks aim to influence borrowing costs. When the central bank reduces the target interest rate, it encourages borrowing and spending, stimulating economic activity. Conversely, when the central bank raises the target interest rate, it discourages borrowing and spending, which helps to control inflation.

Central banks do not have absolute control over interest rates in the long term. Market forces, like supply and demand for credit, also significantly determine interest rates. Central banks can influence short-term rates, but long-term rates are influenced by investors' expectations of future economic conditions, inflation, and risk premiums. Critics of central banks sometimes claim that these institutions manipulate interest rates to benefit certain groups or artificially inflate or deflate asset prices. However, central banks typically operate under a mandate to promote the country's overall economic well-being and aim to create stable and sustainable financial conditions. Their decisions are based on careful analysis of economic indicators, market conditions, and the long-term interests of the economy as a whole.

While central banks can influence interest rates, the notion that they manipulate rates arbitrarily or for their own gain is a myth. Their actions are guided by their mandate to achieve specific economic objectives, and interest rate decisions are made based on careful analysis and consideration of various factors.

3. The central bank is a 'private' or 'public' institution.

Different political perspectives often portray central banks as private or public institutions, but neither perspective provides a balanced view of their role in the monetary system. Understanding the central bank's existence requires knowledge of the financial panics that plagued the global banking systems in the late 1800s and early 1900s, causing severe recessions. The National Banking Acts in the US and their counterparts in other parts of the world addressed some issues but failed to address liquidity problems during crises. The 1907 banking crisis highlighted the need for a central clearinghouse, leading to the establishment of the Federal Reserve System in 1913. Other central banks followed suit soon after.

Central banks have both public and private components. They have a board of governors, a feature that shapes monetary policy, regulates the financial services industry, and oversees the payment system. The system also includes several regional reserve banks owned by private member banks, serving as a "bank for bankers." However, the private banks have limited control over the regional banks, with shares of non-tradeable stock providing a modest dividend and lacking complete control over leadership appointments.

The central bank is often seen as conflicted because it operates through the banking system while promoting maximum employment and price stability. As a result, the central bank is a lender of last resort and aids private banks to ensure a healthy banking system, potentially creating a conflict of interest. This hybrid nature of the central bank has led to its classification as neither purely public nor purely private. It serves both the public and private sectors, with elements of ownership that make it a blend of public and private. Those who present extreme perspectives of the central bank usually have political agendas to promote.

4. We should do away with the central bank.

Recent years have seen many calls to do away with the central bank. Often, this is based on the idea that the central bank manipulates the economy and distorts the 'real' price of financial assets and the price of everyday goods and services. These concerns are not wholly unwarranted, but we don't want to do away with central banks. This myth overlooks the crucial role central banks play in the functioning of modern economies. There are several reasons why the myth is flawed. For starters, central banks are responsible for implementing monetary policy, which involves managing the money supply, influencing interest rates, and stabilizing the economy. They have the tools to address economic imbalances, control inflation, and promote economic growth. Managing these critical aspects of the economy would be challenging without a central bank.

Secondly, central banks play a crucial role in maintaining financial stability. They monitor and regulate banks and financial institutions to prevent excessive risk-taking, ensure the financial system's integrity, and safeguard depositor funds. Removing central banks could result in greater economic instability, as no independent authority oversees the banking sector. Thirdly, central banks act as lenders of last resort during financial crises or liquidity shortages. They provide liquidity to banks and financial institutions, preventing widespread bank failures and economic disruptions. Financial crises could escalate without a central bank fulfilling this role, leading to severe economic downturns.

Fourthly, central banks often manage exchange rates to ensure international trade and investment stability. They intervene in currency markets to prevent excessive volatility and maintain competitive exchange rates. Eliminating central banks could lead to volatile exchange rates, making it harder for businesses to engage in international trade and investment. Finally, central banks have significant research and analytical capabilities, providing valuable insights into economic trends, risks, and policy implications. They contribute to informed decision-making and guide policymakers, financial institutions, and the public. Removing central banks would result in losing this expertise, making it more challenging to understand and navigate complex economic dynamics.

While central banks are not perfect and can face criticism, advocating for their elimination overlooks their essential role in maintaining economic stability, managing monetary policy, and preserving the financial system's integrity. Rather than abolishing central banks, efforts should improve their transparency, accountability, and effectiveness in fulfilling their mandates.

5. Central banks do not get audited.

The myth that central banks are not audited is not valid. Central banks undergo regular audits to ensure transparency and accountability in their operations. They are subject to external audits conducted by independent auditors or audit institutions. Reputable accounting firms or government bodies typically carry out these audits. They assess the central bank's financial statements, transactions, and overall financial health and ensure its activities comply with relevant accounting standards and regulations.

Central banks also have internal audit departments or units that perform ongoing audits of the bank's operations. These internal audits focus on risk management practices, checking internal controls, and compliance with policies and procedures. Internal auditors provide independent evaluations of the central bank's activities and report their findings to the bank's management and governing bodies. Moreover, since central banks understand the importance of transparency and accountability in their operations, they often publish annual reports that include detailed financial statements, information on monetary policy decisions, and explanations of their activities. These reports are availed to the public and undergo scrutiny from various stakeholders, including financial analysts, academics, and policymakers.

In many countries, central banks operate under a legal framework that outlines their responsibilities and governance structure. Governments often have oversight mechanisms to ensure the central bank's adherence to its mandate and to review its performance. Parliamentary committees or government agencies may conduct regular reviews or audits of the central bank's activities. Besides, central banks are encouraged to adhere to international standards and best practices in financial reporting and auditing. Organizations like the International Monetary Fund (IMF) and the Bank for International Settlements (BIS) provide guidance and promote good governance practices for central banks. Adherence to these standards often requires regular audits and reporting to ensure transparency and accountability.

In truth, central banks are audited externally and internally to ensure transparency, accountability, and compliance with applicable regulations. The myth that central banks are not audited is unfounded, as they are subject to rigorous audits by independent external auditors, have internal audit departments, publish annual reports, and are subject to government oversight.

6. Central banks are omnipotent.

A significant amount of mainstream economics stems from the idea that central banks are extremely powerful as policymakers. Perhaps it is good that the recent financial crises have shed some doubt on this myth, even though it persists. Some people became less convinced of the omnipotence of the central bank after seeing some interventions prove ineffectual. They saw that even the central bank is limited regarding its transmission mechanisms for impacting the private sector. For example, when the Fed adjusts interest rates, even though they are altering loan rates for banks, private sector lenders still control their lending rates, which means the central banks do not have ultimate control over what rates reach retail customers. That is why sometimes the Fed cannot induce borrowing using a policy lever.

Additionally, banks don't lend reserves despite the assumptions economists have made over the years. There is no money multiplier between the reserves and loans made. Changing the reserve amount does not directly impact how banks give out loans. Central banks are not powerless, of course, but they are not as powerful as this myth assumes. They operate within complex economic systems that involve numerous factors, such as fiscal policy, global economic conditions, consumer behavior, and technological advancements. These factors interact in intricate ways, making it difficult for central banks to control and predict the outcomes of their policy measures fully. Various actors influence economic outcomes, including governments, financial institutions, businesses, and individual consumers.

Not only that, but central banks face uncertainties and unexpected events that can disrupt their plans and policies. Economic crises, natural disasters, geopolitical events, and technological disruptions are external factors that significantly impact the economy. Central banks must respond to these events, but their ability to entirely prevent or predict them is limited. They primarily rely on interest rate adjustments and other monetary policy tools to influence economic conditions. However, the effectiveness of these tools varies depending on the specific circumstances and the transmission mechanisms within the economy. In certain situations, such as when interest rates are already low or when the economy is experiencing structural issues, the impact of monetary policy measures may be less potent.

While central banks are granted independence to carry out their mandates, they are also accountable to various stakeholders, such as governments, parliaments, and the public. Central banks must balance their policy decisions with public interest considerations, political pressures, and the need for transparency. This can limit their ability to act unilaterally or without oversight. In today's globalized world, economies are interconnected, and central banks must consider the potential spillover effects of their actions on other countries, further limiting their 'omnipotence.' Monetary policies pursued by one central bank can have ripple effects on exchange rates, capital flows, and financial stability internationally. Central banks need to navigate these interdependencies, which can further constrain their ability to exercise omnipotent control.

While central banks play a vital role in influencing monetary policy and promoting economic stability, they face limitations and constraints in their actions. Economic complexity, unforeseen events, the effectiveness of policy tools, accountability, and global interconnectedness all contribute to the reality that central banks do not possess omnipotent powers.

7. There is a secretive cabal that controls central banks.

According to this persistent myth, a secretive group of organizations or individuals—a cabal—controls different central banks. Other variations of this conspiracy theory will make the cabal a family or group of influential people. Sometimes the cabal is said to control all the central banks in the world. The most common version of this conspiracy theory gives control of all central banks in the world to the Rothschild family. This family is said to use its power to influence the events of the world, adding to the list of slander that's been heaped on the family. The House of Rothschild has also been accused of being responsible for various disasters, including the 9/11 attacks, the Malaysian airliner, the Titanic, and many others.

Admittedly, romanticism is associated with the Rothschild barons as they have been close to many significant historical events. The family started business in the 1700s before setting up shop in Vienna, Naples, Paris, London, and other European cities. They found a lot of success lending money to European governments. With such a resumé, you can see why the conspiracy theorists would leap to claim that the House of Rothschild controls the world's central banks. Our modern age economic anxiety does not help matters.

The Rothschild family is in its seventh generation, and its European banking business is still intact. No one knows what the family is worth, which adds to the mystery. Even so, they do not control central banks. Central banks operate under transparent frameworks governed by laws and regulations and are accountable to various stakeholders, including governments and the public.

8. Only the banking elite benefit from the actions of central banks.

According to this myth, central banks primarily serve the interests of financial institutions and commercial banks, neglecting the needs of the general public. While central banks interact with the banking sector, they have a broader mandate to promote the country's overall economic well-being and financial stability. Their policies and decisions aim to achieve maximum employment, stable prices, and sustainable economic growth, with the beneficiaries of these being the entire population of their respective countries.

THE TRUTH BEHIND SOME OF THE MOST PERSISTENT CONSPIRACY THEORIES

Conspiracy theories capture the public's attention, fueling skepticism and sometimes pushing political agendas. In discussing the eight myths above, we have also set the record straight, but one cannot do enough to separate fact from fiction in an age of information overload. So, here are the truths that have been stretched or distorted in those myths and conspiracy theories:

1. The central bank controls the money supply, and CBDCs are tools for mass control.

The truth within this myth is that central banks are exploring digital currencies as a potential for changing the monetary system. Some concerns for surveillance and privacy are valid, but central banks emphasize the importance of transparency and security in digital payment systems while respecting privacy rights.

2. A cabal controls central banks, and central banks only help the elite.

Central banks are quasi-governmental institutions whose mandates serve every player within an economy. They work independently within government frameworks but without private ownership or control by a secret group. Their decisions are subject to mechanisms for oversight and accountability.

3. Central banks manipulate interest rates to control governments and economies.

All central banks, including the ECB and the Federal Reserve, set interest rates based on policy objectives and economic indicators like employment and price stability. Their job is to promote financial stability. It is not to manipulate governments or meet other ulterior motives.

4. Central banks are omnipotent.

Central banks have the power to influence short-term interest rates. Their interventions can save an economy and the financial system from collapsing. Potential spillover effects, accountability frameworks, economic complexity, and unforeseen events constrain their actions.

Our responsibility as the public is to examine expert analysis and evidence for any theories and discard those that lack substance. Central banks are imperfect institutions, but they operate within established frameworks for our economic good in the service of public welfare. It is crucial to evaluate conspiracy theories and use information from credible sources when talking about the realities of central banking.

THE CHALLENGES OF COMMUNICATING THE ROLE OF CENTRAL BANKS TO THE PUBLIC

Following the significant inflation experienced in the 1970s, many countries granted independence to their central banks, a move that is not without controversy in current times. With central bank independence comes the responsibility for accountability to the legislature and the general public. The need for accountability has become even more crucial due to the contentious public debate surrounding the role of central banks in recent days, changes in central bank mandates, and the introduction of new and complex monetary policy tools. Recognizing this, central banks have made considerable efforts to enhance communication with the general public, a departure from the traditional focus on financial markets.

However, effective communication requires active participation from both the sender and the receiver, and the general public typically possesses limited knowledge and a lack of interest in central bank matters. Despite the efforts made by central banks to communicate with the public, their message often fails to reach the intended audience. Many people are unaware of the current level of inflation, hold biased inflation expectations, are unfamiliar with the central bank's inflation target, and have a limited understanding of monetary policy strategies. For example, Even former European Central Bank policymakers acknowledge the need for significant improvements in communication with the general public.

As central banks intensify their efforts to communicate with the general public, there has been a corresponding increase in scholarly literature on this topic. Approximately 15 years ago, it was noted that "most of the research to date has focused on central bank communication with financial markets. It is time to shift more attention to communication with the general public." Thankfully, that shift is taking place, but many challenges must be overcome.

For starters, there is the technical nature of central banking concepts. Communicating about monetary policy is never simple; you need to find the correct vocabulary to get your message across to a broad audience, breaking down content and notions that are not immediately intuitive but will touch the lives of many. It is even more challenging to communicate in countries that have a diverse population. Some of the lack of knowledge around central bank operations is not for a lack of trying from the central banks. Put 'central bank communication' in a search engine and see the results. There is a lot of communication, but why is it not reaching the public? A lot of it has not been broken down into language that is accessible.

Secondly, central banks have to deal with low public engagement, especially with young people. Many years of stable and low inflation have meant that people have forgotten how alarming a persistent and general rise in price levels can be for society. Some of them have never experienced it. At the same time, many people do not see why too low inflation would be a concern. Today, the young have different anxieties and concerns than price stability. Research shows that young people are concerned with climate change or job uncertainties, having lived through a period where those crises are a reality and on the cusp of another industrial revolution.

These changes in preferences and concerns have affected what young people expect of central banks in the few instances they engage with them. In 2020, the ECB set up systems to gather feedback from the general public as part of a plan to review monetary policy. The listening exercise found that younger people assign high importance to the ECB, considering issues past its traditional mandate for ensuring price stability. Other older respondents thought the ECB should only deal with price stability and leave the other matters to democratically elected bodies. Many respondents across different age groups believed that the ECB should be more active in dealing with societal challenges, with climate change prioritizing issues like employment and growth.

For most people today, inflation relates to asset prices and not necessarily the price of consumption goods. This is part of why few are interested in the central bank's mandate—they fail to see how they are directly impacted. Younger generations are concerned with house prices, which are not part of the consumption basket used by central banks when making their policies.

Thirdly, the research proved that many citizens see central banks as distant and inaccessible institutions. Even when presented with opportunities to invest in government bonds and bills, many US citizens avoid it because they do not see themselves as the people who should invest in them. They still see the central bank as only serving other banks. Finally, it doesn't help their communication efforts that central banks have to battle against conspiracy theories affecting public perception. Some people are introduced to conspiracy theories before interacting with official reports or communication from the central bank. It becomes difficult to win them over after that.

These factors show that central banks must design thoughtful and targeted communication strategies to help the public understand, not to further misunderstanding and misinformation. They must consistently pass simple messages to the general public and nuanced messages to expert audiences. More often than not, there is a trade-off between simplicity and precision. Central banks can target individuals and the general public by communicating in shorter and simpler messages. However, they have to be careful because if the message is too short or too simple, it can lack a degree of precision, which could undermine trust if the actual developments differ from the statements of the central bank.

There are inherent limitations to what can be realistically achieved through communication with the general public. It is unlikely that any nation will transform its citizens into experts in monetary policy. The average person lacks the time and energy to delve deeply into such matters. Furthermore, financial and economic literacy levels are generally low and difficult to enhance. The complexity of the subject matter itself poses a challenge. Given the many concerns that occupy citizens' minds, expecting them to grasp the intricacies of concepts like forward guidance or quantitative easing is unrealistic.

However, despite these constraints, the potential benefits of increased and more effective communication between central banks and the general public are significant enough to warrant pursuit. Such benefits include heightened accountability, greater trust, and increased political support. Central bankers should try to attain these objectives, recognizing that it will not be as straightforward as educating financial markets, but the reward will make it worthwhile.

CONCLUSION

THE CENTRAL BANKERS' DILEMMA

> *"The difficulty lies not so much in developing new ideas as in escaping from old ones."*
>
> — **JOHN MAYNARD KEYNES**

THE BALANCING ACT OF MAINTAINING FINANCIAL STABILITY AND ECONOMIC GROWTH

Joseph Heller's novel *Catch-22* delved into the impossible predicaments faced by people trapped in situations with mutually conflicting or dependent conditions. The concept of catch-22 is an apt description of the current plight of the Federal Reserve (and other central banks) as it grapples with the aftermath of a rapidly evolving global banking crisis while attempting to navigate a "dilemma" posed by Federal Reserve Chairman Jerome Powell. This dilemma demands that the central bank restores financial stability and supports economic growth (through re-establishing price stability and minimizing unemployment), and these two goals sometimes conflict.

The central banker's dilemma refers to the inherent challenge central banks face when attempting to fulfill multiple conflicting objectives. As mentioned earlier, the primary objectives of central banks typically encompass maintaining price stability, achieving sustainable economic growth, and ensuring stability in the financial system. These goals often necessitate trade-offs and policy decisions that may lead to conflicts.

For example, central banks manage a trade-off between growth and inflation. They face the challenge of striking the right balance between controlling inflation and promoting economic growth. Restrictive monetary policies to curb inflation can slow economic activity, while expansionary policies to stimulate growth may fuel inflationary pressures. Imagine a situation where the economy is facing high unemployment and high inflation. In that case, the bank experiences pressure to lower interests and increase the money supply to stimulate economic growth and reduce unemployment, but doing this could exacerbate already high inflation. What is the central banker to do?

Not only that, but central banks also have to navigate the conflict between growth and financial stability. Policies that ensure financial system stability, such as stricter regulations and higher capital requirements, can limit credit availability and potentially hinder economic growth. Conversely, relaxed regulations to spur economic activity may increase the financial system's vulnerability to shocks. Suppose a country experiences a surge in capital inflows. In that case, the central bank has to decide whether to let the domestic currency appreciate, which can make exports less competitive, or institute measures that control currency appreciation. If they choose the latter, it can cause inflationary pressures. As if external and domestic considerations are not severe enough, central banks may face the dilemma of balancing financial stability concerns to promote growth in periods of economic expansion. For example, suppose the housing market overheats with rising asset prices and increasing household debt. The central bank might be torn between tightening monetary policy to prevent a potential housing bubble or maintaining accommodative policies to support overall economic growth.

As they try to balance these conflicts, central banks also have to balance a third aspect, which involves both long-term and short-term considerations—they must also consider the trade-offs between short-term and long-term objectives. While addressing immediate economic challenges may involve accommodating policies, this can have long-term implications, such as the risk of inflation or financial imbalances. For example, when responding to an economic downturn, the central bank might lower interest rates and inject liquidity into the financial system to stimulate immediate economic activity. However, this may create the risk of fostering unsustainable debt levels or asset price bubbles in the long run. Again, during times of financial crisis, central banks face the dilemma of maintaining stability in the financial system while ensuring market confidence. For instance, in the aftermath of a banking crisis, the central bank might be torn between providing liquidity support to troubled financial institutions to prevent systemic risks and the concern of moral hazard or the perception of favoritism toward certain market participants.

The job of the central banker is not clear-cut. Addressing the central banker's dilemma requires a delicate balance and a comprehensive understanding of the economic and financial landscape. Central bankers often employ a mix of monetary policy tools, such as interest rate adjustments, setting reserve requirements, open market operations, forward guidance, and macroprudential measures, to navigate conflicting objectives.

Central banks have the authority to set reserve requirements, determining the minimum reserve amount that commercial banks must hold. By adjusting these requirements, central banks can influence the amount of money that banks can lend and, therefore, control the money supply in the economy. Increasing reserve requirements reduces the funds available for lending, limiting credit expansion and potentially curbing inflation. Secondly, central bankers take part in open market operations. Open market operations involve the buying and selling of government bonds by the central bank in the open market. When the central bank purchases securities, it injects money into the banking system, increasing the money supply. Conversely, selling securities reduces the money supply. By conducting open market operations, central banks can influence short-term interest rates and manage liquidity in the financial system.

Thirdly, central bankers manage their dilemma through interest rate adjustments. They set key interest rates, such as the policy or overnight lending rates. Central banks influence borrowing costs by increasing or decreasing these rates, impacting consumption, investment, and inflation. Raising interest rates helps combat inflationary pressures by making borrowing more expensive, while lowering rates stimulates economic activity and supports growth. Finally, they use forward guidance when the situation calls for it. Forward guidance is a communication tool central banks employ to shape market expectations about future monetary policy decisions. Central banks provide guidance on their future policy intentions, signaling their stance on interest rates, inflation targets, and economic outlook. By managing expectations, central banks can influence market behavior, investment decisions, and long-term interest rates, impacting economic conditions.

Central banks have recently developed additional tools in response to emerging challenges. For example, some central banks have adopted negative interest rates, wherein banks are charged for holding excess reserves. This policy is intended to incentivize lending and discourage the hoarding of cash. Additionally, macroprudential tools have been introduced to address financial stability risks, such as capital buffers, loan-to-value ratios, and stress testing requirements. As discussed in earlier chapters, unconventional monetary policies like quantitative easing also often come in handy. During times of severe economic downturn or financial crises, central banks may implement quantitative easing. The extra infusion of liquidity into the market due to quantitative easing aims to stimulate lending, lower long-term interest rates, and support economic activity. Central banks notably employed quantitative easing in response to the global financial crisis of 2008–2009. The massive rounds of quantitative easing implemented post the market turmoil driven by the 2020 pandemic are thought to have contributed significantly to the soaring inflation in 2022 and 2023.

If central bankers do not do the balancing work, adverse consequences can arise, potentially leading to hyperinflation, economic recession, or financial crises. Hyperinflation occurs when there is an extreme and uncontrollable rise in prices, eroding the purchasing power of money. If central banks prioritize economic growth excessively and engage in overly expansionary monetary policies, such as excessively low interest rates or excessive money printing, it can fuel inflationary pressures. The resulting hyperinflationary environment leads to a loss of confidence in the currency, economic instability, and severe hardships for individuals and businesses. A notable historical example is the hyperinflation experienced in Zimbabwe during the late 2000s. The government pursued unsustainable economic policies, including excessive money printing, which led to hyperinflation, eroded the value of the Zimbabwean dollar, and caused economic turmoil.

If too much emphasis is placed on financial stability, central banks may adopt overly restrictive monetary policies to combat inflation or maintain exchange rate stability. This can result in a slowdown in economic activity, leading to an economic recession. Excessively high interest rates or tight credit conditions can hinder business investments, consumer spending, and overall economic growth. An example of this occurred during the subprime mortgage crisis of 2007–2009. Central banks, focused on financial stability, initially tightened monetary policy to combat inflationary pressures. However, this inadvertently exacerbated the crisis as the tight credit conditions contributed to a severe economic downturn, resulting in recessions across many countries.

Weighty emphasis on economic growth without adequate consideration for financial stability can lead to the buildup of financial imbalances, speculative bubbles, and vulnerabilities within the financial system. When these imbalances eventually unravel, they can trigger financial crises with severe economic consequences. The subprime mortgage crisis is such an example. Pursuing economic growth and increased homeownership led to lax lending standards and the proliferation of complex financial products. When the housing bubble burst, it triggered a chain reaction of defaults, bank failures, and a broader financial crisis, ultimately leading to a global recession.

An imbalance in prioritizing either financial stability or economic growth can have significant repercussions. Hyperinflation can erode the value of money and create economic instability; economic recessions can result from overly restrictive policies, and financial crises can emerge when financial stability concerns are ignored. Central banks must strike a delicate balance between these objectives, implementing appropriate policies to avoid such imbalances and mitigate the associated risks. This is one of the primary reasons the central bank needs to be independent. When central banks have a high degree of independence from political interference, they can make objective and effective decisions that prioritize the long-term interests of the economy over short-term political considerations. Political pressures can jeopardize this delicate balance, leading to suboptimal outcomes such as inflationary pressures, financial imbalances, and short-sighted policies. Upholding the independence of central banks strengthens their ability to make objective decisions, enhances credibility, and fosters long-term economic stability.

Central banks will likely face several challenges and opportunities in balancing financial stability and economic growth. One of these challenges may have to do with climate change. The increasing frequency and severity of climate-related events can lead to physical risks like property damage and supply chain disruptions and transition risks such as stranded assets and policy changes that affect the stability of financial systems. Central banks must assess and manage these risks, incorporating climate-related factors into their financial regulation, stress testing, and risk management frameworks.

It is also possible that the proliferation of cryptocurrencies, such as Bitcoin and Ethereum, will pose a challenge for central banks. These digital currencies operate outside the traditional banking system and can potentially impact financial stability, monetary policy transmission, and control of the money supply. Central banks are exploring the potential risks and benefits associated with cryptocurrencies and exploring the development of central bank digital currencies as a way to maintain control over monetary policy and financial stability in the digital era.

It is also possible that as economies become more interconnected, central banks will face challenges in managing cross-border capital flows, exchange rate stability, and spill-over effects. Global financial integration can amplify financial vulnerabilities and the transmission of shocks across countries. Central banks need to strengthen coordination and cooperation, engaging in dialogue and information sharing to enhance the resilience of the global financial system and minimize systemic risks.

Fortunately, the complex and interconnected nature of the global economy will necessitate enhanced cooperation among central banks. Collaborative efforts in sharing information, coordinating policies, and establishing common frameworks may improve the effectiveness of measures taken to ensure financial stability and promote sustainable economic growth.

The central banker's dilemma highlights the intricate challenges central banks face when pursuing multiple objectives simultaneously. Balancing price stability, economic growth, and financial system stability necessitates careful consideration of trade-offs and potential conflicts. By employing appropriate policy tools and effective communication strategies, central banks strive to mitigate this dilemma, aiming to steer economies toward sustainable and prosperous outcomes. While the task faced by central bankers is undoubtedly complex, it is essential to recognize that achieving this balance is fundamental to sustainable economic growth and financial stability. Price stability helps maintain the purchasing power of money and fosters confidence in the economy. Simultaneously, economic growth supports job creation, income growth, and overall prosperity. That is to say; for sustainable economic growth, maintaining price stability, and safeguarding the well-being of individuals and businesses, we need central bankers to perform the balancing act.

THE FUTURE OF CENTRAL BANKING AND ITS IMPACT ON THE WORLD ECONOMY

The global economy has been changing. After the 2020 pandemic, the weaponization of energy, Russia's war against Ukraine, a sudden acceleration in inflation, and a growing rivalry between China and the US, the geopolitical environment is changing fast. The global economy is becoming fragmented into competing blocs, and each one is trying to gain the support of the rest of the world. Each is working harder to get the rest of the world closer to its strategic interests. This fragmentation could coalesce around unions led by the largest economies in the world. If this happened, it could have incredible implications across many domains of central banking, including policymaking. The global economy could become more unstable with a waning global supply, and multipolarity could grow alongside growing geopolitical tensions.

During the Cold War, the world enjoyed a favorable geopolitical climate. Under the leadership of the US, international institutions that abode rules flourished, as did global trade. This created a deepening of global value chains. When China became part of the world economy, there was a significant upturn in labor supply worldwide. Because of that, global supply became more yielding to changes in domestic demand, creating a period of low and stable inflation. In turn, that underpinned a framework for a policy where independent central banks could channel all their energies toward stabilizing inflation by guiding demand without having to think so much about the supply side of the equation.

It seems that that period is now ending, and we are entering one of lasting instability that may create higher costs, lower growth, and uncertain trade partnerships. Rather than an elastic global supply, there is a risk of repeated supply shocks. Events in the recent past have made it clear how much supply depends on a stable global economy more than any other place that has been visible in the energy crisis in Europe. As of 2023, the US depends on imports for more than ten critical minerals. Europe gets 98% of its rare earth supply from China. Disruption of these supplies could affect major sectors of the economy, like the automobile industry.

Governments are beginning to legislate to increase supply security to respond to these issues. In the US, there is the Inflation Reduction Act and the strategic autonomy agenda in Europe. That move could speed up fragmentation as firms also change how they operate in anticipation. Following the Russian invasion of Ukraine, the share of firms in the world that are planning to make their supply chains regional has increased from about 32% to 45% of all global firms. Some economists refer to this as a new global map. Whatever you call it, it would have significant implications for central banks.

A recent study analyzing data since 1900 reveals that geopolitical risks have historically resulted in high inflation, decreased economic activity, and a decline in international trade. The European Central Bank (ECB) also indicates that similar outcomes may be expected in the future. If global value chains become fragmented along geopolitical lines, it is projected that consumer prices globally could rise by approximately 5% in the short term and around 1% in the long term. These changes imply a shift toward a more multipolar world, signifying a second transformation in the central banking landscape.

During Pax Americana after 1945, the US dollar solidified its position as the global reserve and transaction currency, with the euro subsequently rising to second place. This mainly had positive implications for central banks. For instance, central banks could act as the "conductor of the international orchestra," as stated by Keynes, and firms could invoice in their domestic currencies, contributing to price stability for imports. Simultaneously, Western payment infrastructures took on an increasingly global role. For example, in the decade following the fall of the Berlin Wall, the number of countries utilizing the SWIFT payment messaging network more than doubled. By 2020, over 90% of cross-border transmissions were being facilitated through SWIFT. However, new trade patterns may affect payment systems and international currency reserves.

In recent decades, China has significantly increased its bilateral trade in goods with emerging markets and developing economies, becoming the world's top exporter. Research indicates a notable correlation between a country's trade with China and its renminbi holdings as reserves. New trade patterns could also lead to the formation of new alliances. One study demonstrates that unions can raise a partner country's currency reserve holdings by approximately 30 percentage points.

These developments present an opportunity for certain countries seeking to reduce their reliance on Western payment systems and currency frameworks. Motivations for this shift may include political preferences, financial dependencies, or past experiences with economic sanctions over the past decade. Anecdotal evidence, including official statements, suggests that some countries plan to increase their use of alternatives to major traditional currencies for international trade invoicing, such as the Chinese renminbi or the Indian rupee. Additionally, an increasing number of countries, more of those with closer geopolitical ties to China and Russia, are accumulating gold as an alternative reserve asset.

There are also efforts underway to establish alternatives to SWIFT. Russia has developed its own domestic and cross-border use system. Likewise, China has implemented its own payment clearing system for renminbi transactions. While these changes do not suggest an immediate loss of dominance for the US dollar or the euro, they may point to a different future. Currently, the data does not show significant shifts in the use of international currencies. However, it highlights the importance of not taking international currency status for granted.

One wonders how central banks are to respond to these issues. History has given us clear examples of approaches that do not work when there is a sudden increase in volatility. In the 1970s, faced with geopolitical changes, when OPEC stood its ground more, and energy prices started fluctuating, central banks were challenged to act. They failed to offer an anchor for monetary stability, and expectations for inflation fell, a mistake that need not be repeated because now central banks are independent. Their mandates are more explicit than they were back then. When dealing with persistent shocks in supply, independent central banks will need to ensure price stability. However, this can be reached if policies are cooperative and geared toward replenishing supply.

If, for instance, fiscal and structural policies prioritize the elimination of supply constraints resulting from changing geopolitics, such as creating robust supply chains and diversifying energy production, a positive cycle of lower volatility, reduced inflation, increased investment, and higher economic growth could come up. However, suppose fiscal policy primarily focuses on supporting incomes to counterbalance cost pressures without dealing with the underlying issues. In that case, it will likely raise inflation, escalate borrowing costs, and impede investment.

In light of the potential fragmentation of the global economy, it becomes imperative to enhance coherent policy. This does not mean compromising independence but rather acknowledging the interdependence among policies and aligning them toward a strategic goal to maximize their effectiveness. Europe, in particular, stands to benefit from this approach. The multiplier effect of concerted action in industrial policy, defense, and green and digital technologies investments is significantly higher than individual member states acting alone.

Furthermore, achieving the appropriate policy framework not only determines the domestic performance of our economies but also influences how they are perceived globally in the context of heightened "system competition." While the international institutions established after Bretton Woods play a crucial role in fostering a rules-based multilateral order, the emergence of multipolarity raises the stakes for internal policy cohesion.

For example, maintaining an economic policy mix that generates less volatile growth and inflation is vital to attract international investment. Although a significant portion of short-term foreign-held US assets (50–60%) is controlled by governments with strong ties to the United States, making them unlikely to be divested for geopolitical reasons, the fundamental strength of economies remains the most influential factor in determining international currency usage. Likewise, Europe must prioritize long-overdue initiatives such as deepening and integrating its capital markets, which should not be approached solely from the perspective of domestic financial policy. Completing the European capital markets union is crucial in determining whether the euro will continue to be one of the leading global currencies or if others will take its place.

Here, central banks have a critical role, even as protagonists. For example, how we use swap lines could influence dynamics for major currencies worldwide. While operating within their mandates, the ECB and the Fed have proactively provided offshore liquidity in recent crises. However, others are moving, and that's consistent with a growth of the value and role of their currencies. It has already been mentioned that the People's Bank of China created more than 30 bilateral swap lines with central banks worldwide to make up for the lack of liquid markets in the renminbi. The way central banks proceed in the digital era—like issuing CBDCs or innovating their payment systems—will be critical for the currencies that ultimately rise.

The developed world needs to be ready for a new reality in the future, and the time to plan a response to changing geopolitics is now. Central banks in the Americas and Europe will have to offer stability in an age that is nothing but unstable. Hopefully, they will measure up to the challenge.

THE FUTURE OF CENTRAL BANKING IN AFRICA

To discuss the future of central banking in Africa, we must look at its current state and the dominant challenges for central bankers as they try to deal with the increasingly complex forces of a global economy for emerging and underdeveloped economies. I will briefly take stock of the developments in monetary policy and banking in the last several decades as they affect Africa. Historically, the main objectives of monetary policy have been to uphold price and financial stability and to contribute to full employment. Occasionally, there may seem to be a conflict between the goals of low inflation and economic growth. However, we have learned from past experiences that high inflation distorts the private sector's decisions on savings and investment, ultimately leading to slower growth.

Consequently, countries have increasingly placed greater importance on price stability, with many making low and stable inflation their primary objective for monetary policy. To achieve this goal, monetary policy frameworks have evolved over time. Following the Second World War, economic policy operated within the framework of fixed exchange rates under the Bretton Woods system. After the collapse of this system in 1972, central banks generally adopted monetary targets and soft exchange rate pegs to combat the high inflation experienced globally until the early 1980s. However, as inflation subsided and financial innovation emerged, the connection between monetary targets and inflation outcomes became less reliable. Furthermore, the rise in capital flows and the resulting market volatility presented significant challenges for small, open economies that relied on soft exchange rate pegs to manage external shocks while pursuing price stability.

Consequently, central banks gradually transitioned to forward-looking monetary policy frameworks to stabilize their economies. Beginning with New Zealand in 1989, many central banks responded to these challenges by adopting formal inflation targeting as a monetary policy framework. This approach involves setting an explicit inflation target and committing to using market-based instruments and a flexible exchange rate to achieve the target over the medium term.

Although not all central banks adopted formal inflation targeting frameworks, most employed similar operational frameworks centered around adjusting short-term policy rates to maintain low and stable inflation over the medium term. These forward-looking monetary policy frameworks were supported by legislative mandates that granted central banks operational independence. Additionally, procedures were set up to ensure central bank transparency and public accountability. These trends have influenced central banking in Sub-Saharan Africa. Immediately after independence, their governments controlled the new central banks and were directed to finance large amounts of debt. There were unwelcome interest rate and foreign exchange controls.

Toward the end of the 1980s, the region adopted policy frameworks based on exchange rate pegs or monetary targets. These resulted in smaller fiscal deficits and had the central banks financing less of those deficits. Today, however, there is a weaker relationship between inflation and money supply, calling for African central banks to change how they operate. Uganda, South Africa, and Ghana have taken up formal inflation-targeting regimes. Other African countries whose exchange rate regimes are flexible have started reducing the role of monetary aggregates and adding elements of policy practices from emerging and industrial market countries. Some have started relying more on interest rates to transmit monetary policy stances and improve liquidity management, for example.

In Kenya, there is no formal target for inflation. Still, for a decade, the country has adopted a forward-looking policy framework grounded on the CBK's policy rate that a policy committee sets. This policy aims to maintain inflation within the target range for the government, at 2.5% on either side of the 5% target. With this framework, Kenya has managed to keep inflation within the targeted range most of the time. The shift toward futuristic monetary frameworks in Sub-Saharan Africa has been supported by lowered fiscal deficits, intensive use of monetary instruments, and more elastic exchange rate regimes.

Concurrently, financial systems in Africa have deepened in the last decade, which should mean more robust monetary transmission in the future. It has helped that the region emerged as a world leader in innovation around financial services based on mobile phone technology, creating a breakthrough in inclusion, especially in East Africa. Kenya has been paving the way in this, with more than 75% of the population having financial access, thanks to the spread of services like M-Kesho, M-Pesa, and M-Shwari, which have facilitated personal transactions at lower costs. Kenya also has a diverse financial sector, with a well-established bond market, offering support for effective monetary policy transmission. Other countries in Africa are seeing similar progress.

Even so, many African central banks must face serious obstacles as they develop and implement policies. Many African nations have been grappling with the consequences of plummeting commodity prices. Economic growth has experienced a significant decline, and inflation is surging due to the depreciation of exchange rates. While countries like Kenya, less reliant on commodity exports, are faring better, their central banks find their flexibility increasingly limited. This can be attributed to the region's integration into global trade and financial networks, making them subject to forces beyond their control.

One notable factor contributing to this predicament is the uncertainty surrounding withdrawing from unconventional monetary policies in advanced economies. This uncertainty has heightened the volatility of capital flows. The concern is that a sudden reversal of capital inflows could trigger a substantial and disorderly depreciation of the local currency, negatively impacting inflation and financial stability. These circumstances significantly complicate the implementation of monetary policy. Nevertheless, there is a positive aspect as many central banks in Sub-Saharan Africa have built substantial international reserves. Kenya's central bank, the CBK, is included in this category, granting them superior maneuverability and reducing the risk of abrupt capital flow reversals.

The convergence of global developments exacerbates the domestic challenges central banks face. Many of them still have limitations in their operational capacity. This is partially due to ongoing weaknesses in government cash flow management, making it challenging for central banks to manage liquidity conditions effectively. Furthermore, restrictions on accessing central bank lending facilities and deposit placement with the central bank often result in significant disparities between policy rates and market rates relevant to commercial bank liquidity management. This situation undermines the relevance of policy rates for commercial bank pricing and lending decisions, thus diminishing the efficacy of monetary policy.

Another pressing issue in many African countries is the persistent existence of substantial interest rate spreads between deposit rates and loan rates. This has understandably led borrowers to express frustration regarding the cost of credit and has prompted calls for interest rate controls. However, it is essential to recognize the risks associated with politicizing monetary policy, particularly regarding the soundness of the financial system and credit access, especially for higher-risk borrowers. International experience suggests that interest rate controls often lead to reduced access to the banking system for small borrowers, such as farmers, SMEs, and consumers. Furthermore, they may revive informal lending with significantly higher costs for borrowers.

Additionally, linking deposit and lending rates to the central bank's policy rate may compromise its independence and impede its ability to implement monetary policy effectively. This undermines its primary objectives of maintaining price and financial stability while supporting the economy. The limitations of economic indicators in most countries, especially on the real economy and external trade, constrain authorities from taking timely corrective action. The answers to these challenges and, therefore, the future of these central banks will differ from country to country.

Countries that have decided to be part of a currency union or to keep a hard peg will have their exchange rate anchor policy. Other countries with weak institutional capacity will need to build capacity first. For many others, though, futuristic policy frameworks will become necessary, mainly the frontier economies, which are becoming more integrated into the global financial markets. African central banks will prioritize having clear legal mandates for policy goals and the independence to go after those goals. Their primary policy will be price stability, and they will seek to increase their capability to influence variables like output growth. You will likely see transparent objectives for inflation within these central banks as a benchmark for measuring performance.

The African central bank needs to carefully account for the implications of making any adjustments to monetary policy on financial stability, but this should not be at the expense of its inflation objective. Anything that significantly erodes its credibility has the potential to change inflation expectations negatively, and this could create undesirable results and affect financial stability. These central banks must be clear on how they operate, set operational targets, and communicate how these targets are connected to the medium-term inflation objective. That is how money markets function.

As mentioned, each country deals with unique challenges and conditions that determine the pace at which they move into the future. The necessary thing to remember is to have internally consistent goals for policies and arrangements within the institution that allows for independence of the central bank in pursuit of its objectives and to support transparency. Some African countries have already advanced along this path. Hopefully, others will follow.

LOOKING FORWARD: INDIA AND THE PHILIPPINES

For most parts of Asia, the ideal of a genuinely independent central bank is still a distant aspiration. However, central banks are still the most vital institutions in the region, even though they are not entirely independent. They can still exercise independence in setting the financial framework and monetary policy. This has built credibility and anchored the public's expectations for the economy's direction and prices. In Asia, central banks should not be able to be swayed by political pressure, but that is what is happening in the Philippines and India, and the consequences of this may be debilitating.

India's Reserve Bank is among the country's great institutions, ranked several times alongside the Armed Forces and the Election Commission as public bodies most trusted by the public. It is located in Mumbai, which helps as the RBI strives to build its reputation as separate from political decision-makers. Yet, that reputation has never seemed further from being achievable, especially after the finance ministry in India replaced former governor Urjit Patel with Shaktikanta Das, a bureaucrat who seems to have views on financial and monetary policy that align with the Prime Minister's government.

RBI has seen three governors in a little over five years. Raghuram Rajan's term was not renewed in 2016, and Urjit Patel served for just over two years. Rajan and Patel have PhDs in economics from prestigious Ivy League institutions and gained experience at the International Monetary Fund (IMF). In contrast, the current governor, Shaktikanta Das, comes from the generalist tradition of the Indian bureaucracy.

In the Philippines, President Rodrigo Duterte recently appointed Benjamin Diokno, his budget secretary, as the new governor of the Bangko Sentral ng Pilipinas (BSP), the country's central bank. Like the RBI, the BSP has always been led by a career central banker or an individual with financial sector experience. President Duterte could have chosen one of the BSP's deputy governors, but his decision to appoint a cabinet member fueled suspicions that the government wants greater control over monetary policy.

Concerns about the BSP's independence arise not from Diokno's qualifications (he holds a doctorate in economics and is a prominent academic) but from his close political proximity to President Duterte. These developments in the RBI and BSP raise broad concerns that have implications for the credibility of monetary and financial policy. The first one has to do with the centralization of power. Prime Minister Modi and President Duterte are known for centralizing political power. The relative independence central banks and bankers enjoyed may not sit well with them. Raghuram Rajan gained significant public attention during his tenure as RBI governor, rivaling the prime minister's pronouncements. Leaders like Modi and Duterte might resent the rise of the central bank as an alternative power center.

Secondly, there are legitimate concerns about the political capture of the RBI and BSP. Under Governor Das, the RBI approved a $4 billion interim dividend payment to the central government. This payment helped narrow India's fiscal deficit and created fiscal space for increased social spending ahead of parliamentary elections. The previous governor, Urjit Patel, reportedly refused to approve the dividend payment, eventually leading to his exit. It is early days for Governor Diokno, but any deviation from existing policy will raise concerns.

Thirdly, there are worries regarding the future direction of monetary policy in India and the Philippines. Like President Trump's criticism of the Federal Reserve Board for raising interest rates, Modi and Duterte have hinted that they view monetary policy decisions as political rather than purely technical. Maintaining price stability, managing inflation expectations, and determining appropriate currency levels are core objectives for central banks like the RBI and BSP, which have performed well in these areas. Injecting politics into monetary policy decisions will concern financial markets and confuse the general public. Thailand's central bank and Finance Ministry have been embroiled in a prolonged public dispute over the direction of interest rates, illustrating the increasing political pressures central banks face.

Finally, more so than the Philippines, India faces concerns over bank supervision and the financial services industry. The collapse of Infrastructure Leasing and Financial Services (IL&FS), a significant infrastructure finance provider, has worsened liquidity conditions and made capital scarce for companies in need. This issue compounds ongoing challenges faced by India's state-owned banks, which require a capital infusion of over $40 billion. An independent central bank, free from political considerations, could impartially address these financial challenges.

Asia's impressive economic success is not a mere coincidence; it is built on robust macroeconomic policies that grant central banks the policy space to determine the future direction of monetary policy. However, with politics increasingly influencing central banks in New Delhi,

Manila, and elsewhere, these institutions risk becoming part of the problem rather than the solution to the region's economic challenges.

Thank you for investing your time in reading *A Brief History of Central Banking: How the Quest for Financial Stability Led to Unconventional Monetary Practices*. It has been my pleasure to guide you through the intricate and fascinating world of central banking and its evolution.

Your feedback is incredibly valuable to me. Not only does it help me understand my readers' perspectives and improve my future work, but it also assists other potential readers in deciding whether this book is right for them.

It would mean the world to me if you could **spare a few minutes to leave a review** on your preferred platform. Your honest thoughts can make a significant difference, whether positive, critical, or both. No matter how brief or detailed, every review helps.

OTHER BOOKS BY DOMINIC HAYNES

(AVAILABLE ON AMAZON & AUDIBLE)

A Brief History of Ukraine: A Singular People Within the Crucible of Empires

A Brief History of Western Philosophy: Unraveling the Secrets of Time, the Mind, and Existence

A Brief History of Portugal: Blazing the Trail of a Voyage-Shaped Nation

REFERENCES

Aneja, R., & Dygas, R. (2022). Literature review regarding digital currencies and cryptocurrencies in the new global financial system. *Digital Currencies and the New Global Financial System,* 1-16. https://doi.org/10.4324/9781003310365-1.

Baeriswyl, R., Cornand, C., & Ziliotto, B. (2018). *Observing and shaping the market: The dilemma of central banks.*

Ball, L. M. (2018). *The Fed and Lehman Brothers: Setting the record straight on a financial disaster*. Cambridge University Press.

Bateman, B. W., & Johannsen, B. K. (2013). Rethinking the monetarist experience: Monetary theory and monetary policy in the United States. *HISTORY OF ECONOMIC THOUGHT AND POLICY,* (1), 161-179. https://doi.org/10.3280/spe2013-001009.

Beaudry, P., Carter, T. J., & Lahiri, A. (2022). *Looking through supply shocks versus controlling inflation expectations: Understanding the Central Bank dilemma.*

Board of Governors of the Federal Reserve System. (1961). *The Federal Reserve System: Purposes and functions.*

Bordo, M. D., & Orphanides, A. (2013). The great inflation: The rebirth of modern central banking. In *undefined*. University of Chicago Press.

Bordo, M., & Landon-Lane, J. (2013). The banking panics in the United States in the 1930s: Some lessons for today. *The Great Depression of the 1930s,* 188-211. https://doi.org/10.1093/acprof:oso/9780199663187.003.0007.

Bruner, R. F., & Carr, S. D. (2009). *The panic of 1907: Lessons learned from the market's perfect storm*. John Wiley & Sons.

Buiter, W. H. (2013). The role of central banks in financial stability: How has it changed? *World Scientific Studies in International Economics,* 11-56. https://doi.org/10.1142/9789814449922_0002.

Caldara, D., Gagnon, E., Martínez-García, E., & Neely, C. J. (2020). Monetary policy and economic performance since the financial crisis. *Federal Reserve Bank of Dallas, Globalization Institute Working Papers, 2020*(399). https://doi.org/10.24149/gwp399.

Chadwick, R. (2005). First civilizations: Ancient Mesopotamia and ancient Egypt. https://doi.org/10.1558/isbn.9781845537203.

Conti-Brown, P., & Conti-Brown, P. (2018). The power and independence of the Federal Reserve. https://doi.org/10.1515/9781400888412.

El-Erian, M. A. (2016). *The only game in town: Central banks, instability, and avoiding the next collapse*. Yale University Press.

Federal Reserve System. (2010). *Encyclopedia of U.S. Political History*. https://doi.org/10.4135/9781608712380.n704.

Financial stability and central banks. (2001). *Financial Stability and Central Banks*, 19-36. https://doi.org/10.4324/9780203519820-7.

Friedman, M., & Schwartz, A. J. (2008). A monetary history of the United States, 1867-1960. https://doi.org/10.1515/9781400829330.

Fukuda, S. (2011). Nontraditional financial policies. *Japanese Economy, 38*(2), 45-78. https://doi.org/10.2753/jes1097-203x380203.

The gold exchange standard. (2005). *Gold Standard In Theory & History*, 195-213. https://doi.org/10.4324/9780203978870-26.

Goodhart, C. A. (1988). *The evolution of central banks*. MIT Press (MA).

Hafer, R. W. (2005). The Federal Reserve System: An encyclopedia. In *undefined*. Greenwood Publishing Group.

Howden, D., & Salerno, J. T. (2014). *The Fed at one hundred: A critical view on the Federal Reserve System*. Springer.

Johnson, J. (2016). *Priests of prosperity: How central bankers transformed the Postcommunist world*. Cornell University Press.

Katsu, E. (2020). Quantitative and qualitative monetary easing, negative interest rates and the stability of the financial system in Japan. *Unconventional Monetary Policy and Financial Stability*, 164-193. https://doi.org/10.4324/9780429032479-10.

Kozińska, M. (2022). Issue of Central Bank digital currencies – potential consequences for the shape of the financial system. *Digital Currencies and the New Global Financial System*, 94-104. https://doi.org/10.4324/9781003310365-8.

Rasmus, J. (2017). *Central bankers at the end of their rope?: Monetary policy and the coming depression*. SCB Distributors.

Richardson, B. (n.d.). *The Great Depression*. Federal Reserve History. https://www.federalreservehistory.org/essays/great-depression.

Temin, P., & Timberlake, R. H. (1979). The origins of central banking in the United States. *The Journal of American History, 66*(2), 391. https://doi.org/10.2307/1900919.

Toma, M. (1986). Inflationary bias of the Federal Reserve System. *Central Bankers, Bureaucratic Incentives, and Monetary Policy*, 37-66. https://doi.org/10.1007/978-94-009-4432-9_3.

Tomšič, M. (2022). Political elites, leadership, and the rise of populism. *The Rise of Populism in Central and Eastern Europe*, 10-23. https://doi.org/10.4337/9781802205534.00008.

Wicker, E. (2000). The banking panics of the Great Depression. In *undefined*. Cambridge University Press.

Wicker, E., & Timberlake, R. H. (1980). The origins of central banking in the United States. *Journal of Money, Credit and Banking, 12*(1), 126. https://doi.org/10.2307/1991604.

Made in the USA
Monee, IL
12 November 2026

e894a114-9f95-4e5e-b4c7-5d3bef3f9c0cR01